I0813837

Salad Today

pil

Publications International, Ltd.

Louis Weber, CEO
Publications International, Ltd.
8140 Lehigh Ave
Morton Grove, IL 60053

Pictured on the front cover: Broccoli and Cauliflower Salad *(page 97).*

Pictured on the back cover *(left to right, top to bottom):* Mediterranean Chopped Salad *(page 37),* Pear Arugula Salad *(page 14),* Green Bean, Walnut and Blue Cheese Pasta Salad *(page 84),* Almond Chicken Salad *(page 136)* and Texas Caviar *(page 120).*

ISBN: 978-1-63938-740-3

Manufactured in China.

8 7 6 5 4 3 2 1

Microwave Cooking: Microwave ovens vary in wattage. Use the cooking times as guidelines and check for doneness before adding more time.

WARNING: Food preparation, baking and cooking involve inherent dangers: misuse of electric products, sharp electric tools, boiling water, hot stoves, allergic reactions, foodborne illnesses and the like, pose numerous potential risks. Publications International, Ltd. (PIL) assumes no responsibility or liability for any damages you may experience as a result of following recipes, instructions, tips or advice in this publication.

While we hope this publication helps you find new ways to eat delicious foods, you may not always achieve the results desired due to variations in ingredients, cooking temperatures, typos, errors, omissions or individual cooking abilities.

Let's get social!

@Publications_International

@PublicationsInternational

www.pilbooks.com

Contents

Side Salads

Beet and Arugula Salad

Makes 6 servings

- 8 medium beets (5 to 6 ounces each)
- ⅓ cup red wine vinegar
- ¾ teaspoon salt
- ½ teaspoon black pepper
- 3 tablespoons extra virgin olive oil
- 1 package (5 ounces) baby arugula
- 1 package (4 ounces) crumbled goat cheese with garlic and herbs

1. Place beets in large saucepan; add water to cover by 2 inches. Bring to a boil over medium-high heat. Reduce heat to medium-low; cover and simmer 30 minutes or until beets can be easily pierced with tip of knife. Drain; set aside until cool enough to handle.
2. Meanwhile, whisk vinegar, salt and pepper in large bowl. Slowly add oil in thin, steady stream, whisking until well blended. Remove 3 tablespoons dressing to medium bowl.
3. Peel beets and cut into wedges. Add warm beets to large bowl; toss to coat with dressing. Add arugula to medium bowl; toss gently to coat with dressing. Place arugula on serving plates; top with beets and cheese.

Fattoush Salad

Makes 4 to 6 servings

- 2 pita bread rounds
- ⅓ cup plus 3 tablespoons olive oil, divided
- 1 teaspoon salt, divided
- 2 cups chopped romaine or green leaf lettuce
- 1 seedless cucumber, quartered lengthwise and sliced
- 2 tomatoes, diced
- 4 green onions, thinly sliced
- 3 radishes, thinly sliced
- ¼ cup finely chopped fresh parsley
- 1 tablespoon finely chopped fresh mint
- 2 tablespoons pomegranate molasses
- 2 cloves garlic, minced
- 2 tablespoons red wine vinegar
- 1 tablespoon lemon juice
- Black pepper

1. Preheat oven to 400°F. Cut pita into 1-inch cubes. Toss with 3 tablespoons oil and ½ teaspoon salt in large bowl. Spread on large baking sheet. Bake 10 minutes or until pita cubes are browned and crisp. Cool completely on baking sheet.
2. Combine lettuce, cucumber, tomatoes, green onions, radishes, parsley and mint in large bowl. Add pita cubes.
3. For dressing, combine remaining ⅓ cup oil, molasses, garlic, vinegar and lemon juice in small bowl. Season with remaining ½ teaspoon salt and pepper; whisk until well blended. Taste and adjust seasoning. Pour over salad; toss until well blended.

Spinach Salad

Makes 8 servings

Dressing

- ¼ cup balsamic vinegar
- 1 clove garlic, minced
- ½ teaspoon sugar
- ¼ teaspoon salt
- ⅛ teaspoon black pepper
- ¼ cup extra virgin olive oil
- ¼ cup vegetable oil

Salad

- 8 cups packed baby spinach
- 1 cup diced tomatoes (about 2 medium)
- 1 cup drained mandarin oranges
- 1 cup glazed pecans, store-bought or homemade (recipe follows)
- ½ cup crumbled feta cheese
- ½ cup diced red onion
- ½ cup dried cranberries
- 1 can (3 ounces) crispy rice noodles*
- 4 teaspoons toasted sesame seeds

**Crispy rice noodles can be found with canned chow mein noodles in the Asian section of the supermarket.*

1 For dressing, whisk vinegar, garlic, sugar, salt and pepper in medium bowl until blended. Slowly whisk in olive oil and vegetable oil until well blended.

2 For salad, combine spinach, tomatoes, oranges, pecans, cheese, onion and cranberries in large bowl. Sprinkle with rice noodles and sesame seeds. Drizzle with dressing; toss to coat.

Glazed Pecans

Combine 1 cup pecan halves, ¼ cup sugar, 1 tablespoon butter and ½ teaspoon salt in medium skillet; cook and stir over medium heat 5 minutes or until sugar mixture is dark brown and nuts are well coated. Spread on large plate; cool completely. Break into pieces or coarsely chop.

Greek Salad

Makes 6 servings

Salad

- 3 medium tomatoes, cut into 8 wedges each
- 1 green bell pepper, cut into 1-inch pieces
- ½ English cucumber (8 to 10 inches), quartered lengthwise and sliced crosswise
- ½ red onion, thinly sliced
- ½ cup pitted Kalamata olives
- 1 block (8 ounces) feta cheese, cut into ½-inch cubes

Dressing

- 6 tablespoons extra virgin olive oil
- 3 tablespoons red wine vinegar
- 1 to 2 cloves garlic, minced
- ¾ teaspoon dried oregano
- ¾ teaspoon salt
- ¼ teaspoon black pepper

1. For salad, combine tomatoes, bell pepper, cucumber, onion and olives in large bowl. Top with feta.
2. For dressing, whisk oil, vinegar, garlic, oregano, salt and black pepper in small bowl until well blended. Pour over salad; stir gently to coat.

Asparagus and Arugula Salad

Makes 4 to 6 servings

- ½ cup sun-dried tomatoes (not packed in oil)
- 1 cup boiling water
- 1 cup sliced asparagus (1-inch pieces)
- ¼ cup extra virgin olive oil
- 2 tablespoons lemon juice
- 1 tablespoon orange juice
- 1 clove garlic, minced
- ½ teaspoon salt
- ½ teaspoon grated lemon peel
- ⅛ teaspoon black pepper
- 1 package (5 ounces) baby arugula (4 cups)
- ½ cup shaved Parmesan cheese

1. Place sun-dried tomatoes in small bowl; cover with boiling water. Let stand 5 minutes; drain well.
2. Bring medium saucepan of salted water to a boil. Add asparagus; cook 1 minute or until crisp-tender. Drain and run under cold water to stop cooking.
3. Whisk oil, lemon juice, orange juice, garlic, salt, lemon peel and pepper in small bowl until well blended.
4. Combine arugula, asparagus, sun-dried tomatoes and cheese in large bowl. Pour dressing over salad; toss gently to coat.

Pear Arugula Salad

Makes 4 servings

Caramelized Pecans

- ½ cup pecan halves
- 3 tablespoons packed brown sugar
- 1 tablespoon butter
- 1 tablespoon honey
- ¼ teaspoon salt
- ⅛ teaspoon ground cinnamon

Dressing

- ¼ cup extra virgin olive oil
- 3 tablespoons balsamic vinegar
- 1 teaspoon pomegranate molasses or honey
- 1 teaspoon Dijon mustard
- ½ teaspoon salt
- ¼ teaspoon dried thyme
- ⅛ teaspoon black pepper

Salad

- 2 cups arugula
- 2 red pears, thinly sliced
- ½ cup crumbled gorgonzola, blue or goat cheese

1 For pecans, preheat oven to 350°F. Line small baking sheet with foil; spray foil with nonstick cooking spray. Combine pecans, brown sugar, butter, honey, ¼ teaspoon salt and cinnamon in medium skillet. Cook and stir 2 to 3 minutes or until sugar and butter are melted and nuts are glazed. Spread on foil. Bake 5 to 7 minutes or until nuts are fragrant and a shade darker. Remove foil from baking sheet; cool nuts completely on foil.

2 For dressing, whisk oil, vinegar, molasses, mustard, ½ teaspoon salt, thyme and pepper in small bowl until smooth and well blended.

3 Divide arugula among four serving plates. Top with pears, nuts and cheese; drizzle with 2 tablespoons dressing.

Wedge Salad

Makes 4 servings

Dressing

- ¾ cup mayonnaise
- ½ cup buttermilk
- 1 cup crumbled blue cheese, divided
- 1 clove garlic, minced
- ½ teaspoon sugar
- ⅛ teaspoon onion powder
- ⅛ teaspoon salt
- ⅛ teaspoon black pepper

Salad

- 1 head iceberg lettuce
- 1 large tomato, diced (about 1 cup)
- ½ small red onion, cut into thin rings
- ½ cup crumbled crisp-cooked bacon (6 to 8 slices)

1 For dressing, combine mayonnaise, buttermilk, ½ cup cheese, garlic, sugar, onion powder, salt and pepper in food processor or blender; process until smooth.

2 For salad, cut lettuce into quarters through stem end; remove stem from each wedge.

3 Place lettuce wedges on individual serving plates; top with dressing. Sprinkle with tomato, onion, remaining ½ cup cheese and bacon.

Italian Salad

Makes 4 servings

Dressing

- ½ cup mayonnaise
- ½ cup white wine vinegar
- ¼ cup grated Parmesan cheese
- 1 tablespoon olive oil
- 1 tablespoon lemon juice
- 1 tablespoon corn syrup
- 1 clove garlic, minced
- ¾ teaspoon Italian seasoning
- ½ teaspoon salt
- ½ teaspoon black pepper

Salad

- 1 package (10 ounces) Italian salad blend
- 2 plum tomatoes, thinly sliced
- 1 cup croutons, store-bought or homemade (recipe follows)
- ½ cup thinly sliced red or green bell pepper
- ½ cup thinly sliced red onion
- ¼ cup sliced black olives
- Pepperoncini peppers (optional)

1 For dressing, whisk mayonnaise, vinegar, cheese, oil, lemon juice, corn syrup, garlic, Italian seasoning, salt and black pepper in medium bowl until well blended.

2 For salad, place salad blend in large bowl; top with tomatoes, croutons, bell pepper, onion, olives and pepperoncini, if desired. Add dressing; toss to coat.

Homemade Croutons

Preheat oven to 350°F. Cut any kind of bread into cubes. Hearty breads like whole wheat, Tuscan or sourdough work best, but sandwich bread works, too. Spread the bread on a large baking sheet and drizzle with olive oil. Toss with spatula or hands to coat. The bread should be evenly coated; add more oil if needed and toss again. If desired, season with salt and pepper and dried herbs like oregano, thyme or rosemary. Bake 10 to 15 minutes or until golden brown, stirring once or twice. Cool on baking sheet before using.

Kale Salad
with Cherries and Avocados

Makes 6 to 8 servings

- **¼ cup plus 1 teaspoon olive oil, divided**
- **3 tablespoons uncooked quinoa**
- **¾ teaspoon salt, divided**
- **3 tablespoons balsamic vinegar**
- **1 tablespoon red wine vinegar**
- **1 tablespoon maple syrup**
- **2 teaspoons Dijon mustard**
- **¼ teaspoon dried oregano**
- **⅛ teaspoon black pepper**
- **1 large bunch kale (about 1 pound)**
- **1 package (5 ounces) dried cherries**
- **2 avocados, diced**
- **½ cup smoked almonds, chopped**

1. Heat 1 teaspoon oil in small saucepan over medium-high heat. Add quinoa; cook and stir 3 to 5 minutes or until quinoa is golden brown and popped. Season with ¼ teaspoon salt. Remove to plate; cool completely.
2. Combine balsamic vinegar, red wine vinegar, maple syrup, mustard, oregano, pepper and remaining ½ teaspoon salt in medium bowl. Whisk in remaining ¼ cup oil until well blended.
3. Place kale in large bowl. Pour dressing over kale; massage dressing into leaves until well blended and kale is slightly softened. Add popped quinoa; stir until well blended. Add cherries, avocados and almonds; toss until blended.

Classic Coleslaw

Makes 10 servings

- 1 medium head green cabbage, shredded
- 1 medium carrot, shredded
- ½ cup mayonnaise
- ½ cup milk
- ⅓ cup sugar
- 3 tablespoons lemon juice
- 1½ tablespoons white vinegar
- 1 teaspoon salt
- ⅛ teaspoon black pepper

1. Combine cabbage and carrot in large bowl; mix well.
2. Whisk mayonnaise, milk, sugar, lemon juice, vinegar, salt and pepper in medium bowl. until well blended. Add to cabbage mixture; stir until blended.

Middle Eastern Spinach Salad

Makes 4 servings

- ¼ cup lemon juice
- 1 tablespoon extra virgin olive oil
- 1 tablespoon packed brown sugar
- ½ teaspoon curry powder
- Salt and black pepper
- 1 pound fresh spinach, stemmed
- ½ cup golden raisins
- ¼ cup minced red onion
- ¼ cup thin red onion slices

1. For dressing, whisk lemon juice, oil, sugar and curry powder in small bowl until blended. Season to taste with salt and pepper.
2. Wash spinach well to remove sand and grit; remove stems and bruised leaves. Drain well; pat dry with paper towels. Tear spinach into bite-size pieces.
3. Combine spinach, raisins, minced onion and onion slices in large bowl. Add dressing; toss gently to coat.

Crunchy Orange-Ginger Slaw

Makes 6 to 8 servings

- **1 package (3 ounces) ramen noodles, coarsely crumbled***
- **1 tablespoon sesame seeds**
- **6 cups finely shredded green cabbage**
- **2 cups shredded carrots**
- **½ cup diced red onion**
- **½ cup raisins**
- **¾ cup orange marmalade**
- **¼ cup cider vinegar**
- **¼ cup vegetable or canola oil**
- **3 tablespoons grated fresh ginger**
- **1 tablespoon soy sauce**
- **1 teaspoon grated orange peel (optional)**
- **1 teaspoon hot pepper sauce *or* ¼ teaspoon red pepper flakes**
- **¼ teaspoon salt**

****Use any flavor; discard seasoning packet.***

1. Heat medium skillet over medium-high heat. Add noodles and sesame seeds; cook 2 minutes or until lightly browned, stirring frequently. Set aside on plate.
2. Combine cabbage, carrots, onion and raisins in large bowl. Whisk marmalade, vinegar, oil, ginger, soy sauce, orange peel, if desired, hot pepper sauce and salt in medium bowl until well blended. Add to cabbage mixture; mix well. Cover and refrigerate at least 20 minutes.
3. Sprinkle with noodle mixture just before serving.

Scallop and Spinach Salad

Makes 4 servings

- 1 package (5 ounces) baby spinach, stemmed
- 3 thin slices red onion, halved and separated
- ½ cup Italian dressing, store-bought or homemade (page 182)
- 12 ounces sea scallops
- ½ teaspoon salt
- ⅛ teaspoon ground red pepper
- ⅛ teaspoon paprika
- 1 tablespoon olive oil
- ¼ cup crumbled blue cheese
- 2 tablespoons toasted walnuts*

*To toast walnuts, cook in small skillet over medium heat 3 to 4 minutes or until lightly browned and fragrant, stirring frequently. Cool before using.

1. Combine spinach, onion and dressing in large bowl; toss to coat.
2. Rinse scallops. Cut in half horizontally to make two thin rounds; pat dry. Season top sides lightly with salt, red pepper and paprika.
3. Heat oil in large nonstick skillet over high heat. Add half of scallops, seasoned sides down, ½ inch apart in single layer. Cook 2 minutes or until browned on bottom. Turn scallops; cook 1 to 2 minutes or until opaque in center. Transfer to plate; cover to keep warm. Repeat with remaining scallops.
4. Divide salad among serving plates. Place scallops on top of spinach; sprinkle with blue cheese and walnuts.

Artisan Salad with Goat Cheese

Makes 6 servings

Balsamic Vinaigrette

- ¼ cup plus 1 tablespoon white balsamic vinegar
- ½ teaspoon minced garlic
- 3 tablespoons extra virgin olive oil
- 12 fresh basil leaves, chopped
- Salt and black pepper

Salad

- 2 packages (5 ounces each) mixed spring greens
- ¾ cup dried cranberries
- ¾ cup toasted chopped walnuts*
- 1 package (4 ounces) soft goat cheese, cut into 6 slices

**To toast walnuts, cook in large skillet over medium heat 3 to 4 minutes or until lightly browned and fragrant, stirring frequently. Cool before using.*

1. Combine vinegar and garlic in small bowl; slowly whisk in oil until well blended. Stir in basil. Season to taste with salt and pepper. Refrigerate at least 1 hour.

2. Toss greens, cranberries and walnuts in large bowl. Add vinaigrette; toss to coat. Divide salads among serving plates; top each serving with one slice of goat cheese.

Spring Greens with Blueberries, Walnuts and Feta Cheese

Makes 4 servings

- 2 tablespoons vegetable or canola oil
- 2 tablespoons white wine vinegar or sherry vinegar
- 2 teaspoons Dijon mustard
- ½ teaspoon salt
- ½ teaspoon black pepper
- 1 package (5 ounces) mixed spring greens
- 1 cup fresh blueberries
- ½ cup (2 ounces) crumbled feta cheese
- ¼ cup chopped walnuts or pecans, toasted*

***To toast walnuts, cook in medium skillet over medium heat 3 to 4 minutes or until lightly browned and fragrant, stirring frequently. Cool before using.*

1. Whisk oil, vinegar, mustard, salt and pepper in large bowl.
2. Add greens and blueberries; toss gently to coat. Top with cheese and walnuts.

Garden Fresh Salad

Makes 4 servings

- 5 cups assorted chopped lettuce
- ½ cup bell pepper slices
- ½ cup cherry or grape tomatoes, quartered or halved
- ½ small cucumber, sliced
- ½ red onion, sliced
- ¼ cup sliced radishes
- Chopped fresh thyme or parsley
- ½ cup salad dressing, store-bought or homemade (see pages 182-187)

1. Combine lettuce, bell pepper, tomatoes, cucumber, onion and radishes in large bowl.
2. Divide salad evenly among individual bowls; top with thyme and dressing.

Beet and Blue Salad

Makes 4 servings

- 1 package (5 ounces) baby spinach
- 1 cup sliced cooked beets
- ½ cup diced red onions
- ½ cup matchstick carrots
- ¼ cup balsamic vinegar
- 2 tablespoons vegetable oil
- 2 tablespoons pure maple syrup
- ¼ teaspoon salt
- ⅛ teaspoon red pepper flakes
- ¼ cup crumbled blue cheese

1 Divide spinach equally among four salad plates. Top evenly with beets, onions and carrots.

2 Whisk vinegar, oil, maple syrup, salt and red pepper flakes in small bowl until well blended. Drizzle dressing over salads. Sprinkle evenly with cheese.

Apple-Walnut Salad
with Blue Cheese-Honey Vinaigrette

Makes 4 servings

- ¼ cup chopped walnuts
- 2 tablespoons white wine vinegar
- 2 tablespoons extra virgin olive oil
- 2 teaspoons honey
- ¼ teaspoon salt
- ⅛ teaspoon black pepper
- ¼ cup crumbled blue cheese
- 1 large head Bibb lettuce, separated into leaves
- 1 Red Delicious or other red apple, thinly sliced
- 1 Granny Smith apple, thinly sliced

1. Place walnuts in small skillet over medium heat. Cook and stir 5 minutes or until fragrant and lightly toasted. Transfer to plate to cool.
2. Whisk vinegar, oil, honey, salt and pepper in small bowl until well blended. Stir in cheese.
3. Divide lettuce and apples evenly among four plates. Drizzle dressing evenly over each salad; top with walnuts.

Entrée Salads

Mediterranean Chopped Salad

Makes 4 servings

- 2 cups chopped iceberg lettuce
- 2 cups baby spinach
- 2 cups diced cucumbers
- 1 cup diced cooked chicken
- 1 cup chopped roasted red peppers
- 1 cup grape tomatoes, halved
- 1 cup quartered artichoke hearts
- ¾ cup crumbled feta cheese
- ½ cup chopped red onion
- 1 cup hummus
- ½ teaspoon Italian seasoning

1. Divide lettuce and spinach among four salad bowls or plates; top with cucumbers, chicken, roasted peppers, tomatoes, artichokes, cheese and onion.
2. Top salads with hummus; sprinkle with Italian seasoning.

Protein Power Salad

Makes 4 servings

Roasted Tomatoes

- 6 plum tomatoes, halved and seeded
- 2 tablespoons olive oil
- 1 tablespoon balsamic vinegar
- Salt and black pepper

Dressing

- ¼ cup balsamic vinegar
- 2 tablespoons honey
- 1 tablespoon Dijon or whole grain mustard
- ½ teaspoon salt
- ¼ teaspoon black pepper
- ½ cup extra virgin olive oil

Salad

- 4 cups baby kale
- 4 cups arugula or spinach
- 1 pouch (about 8 ounces) precooked mixed grains,* prepared according to package directions
- 1 cup drained canned chickpeas
- 1 cup diced cucumber
- 4 hard-cooked eggs (recipe follows), chopped

**Look for a mix of quinoa, barley, millet, flax, brown rice and wild rice.*

1. For tomatoes, preheat oven to 450°F. Line large baking sheet with foil. Arrange tomatoes cut sides up on prepared baking sheet. Drizzle with 2 tablespoons oil and 1 tablespoon vinegar; season lightly with salt and pepper. Roast about 30 minutes or until tomatoes are very soft and slightly charred in spots. Coarsely chop when cool enough to handle.
2. Meanwhile for dressing, whisk ¼ cup vinegar, honey, mustard, ½ teaspoon salt and ¼ teaspoon pepper in medium bowl. Slowly whisk in ½ cup oil until well blended.
3. For each salad, combine 1 cup kale and 1 cup arugula in serving bowl; top with ½ cup grains and ¼ cup chickpeas. Arrange ¼ cup cucumber, one egg and one fourth of roasted tomatoes on greens around grains. Drizzle each salad with 2 to 3 tablespoons dressing.

Hard-Cooked Eggs

Bring large saucepan of water to a boil. Gently lower desired number of eggs into water with slotted spoon; reduce heat to maintain a gentle simmer. Simmer 11 minutes. Meanwhile, fill large bowl with ice and cold water. Drain eggs and place in ice bath; let cool 10 minutes before peeling.

Roasted Brussels Sprouts Salad

Makes 4 to 6 servings

Brussels Sprouts

- 1 pound Brussels sprouts, trimmed and halved
- 2 tablespoons olive oil
- ½ teaspoon salt

Salad

- 2 cups coarsely chopped baby kale
- 2 cups coarsely chopped romaine lettuce
- 1½ cups candied pecans*
- 1 cup halved red grapes
- 1 cup diced cucumbers
- ½ cup dried cranberries
- ½ cup fresh blueberries
- ½ cup chopped red onion
- ¼ cup toasted pumpkin seeds (pepitas)
- 1 container (4 ounces) crumbled goat cheese

Dressing

- ½ cup extra virgin olive oil
- 6 tablespoons balsamic vinegar
- 6 tablespoons strawberry jam
- 2 teaspoons Dijon mustard
- 1 teaspoon salt

***Candied or glazed pecans may be found in the produce section of the supermarket with other salad toppings, or they may be found in the snack aisle.**

1. For Brussels sprouts, preheat oven to 400°F. Spray large baking sheet with nonstick cooking spray.
2. Combine Brussels sprouts, 2 tablespoons oil and ½ teaspoon salt in medium bowl; toss to coat. Arrange Brussels sprouts in single layer, cut sides down, on prepared baking sheet. Roast 20 minutes or until tender and browned, stirring once halfway through roasting. Cool completely on baking sheet.
3. For salad, combine kale, lettuce, pecans, grapes, cucumbers, cranberries, blueberries, onion and pumpkin seeds in large bowl. Top with Brussels sprouts and cheese.
4. For dressing, whisk ½ cup oil, vinegar, jam, mustard and 1 teaspoon salt in small bowl until well blended. Pour dressing over salad; toss gently to coat.

Quinoa and Cauliflower Taco Salad

Makes 6 servings

- ¾ cup uncooked quinoa
- 1½ cups water
- 4 cloves garlic, minced, divided
- 1 tablespoon chili powder
- 1¾ teaspoons salt, divided
- 1¼ teaspoons ground cumin, divided
- ½ teaspoon dried oregano
- ¼ cup plus 2 teaspoons extra virgin olive oil, divided
- 4 cups coarsely chopped cauliflower
- ½ cup raw pepitas (pumpkin seeds)
- Juice of 1 lime
- Salt and black pepper
- 4 to 6 cups shredded iceberg lettuce
- 2 tomatoes, diced
- 2 avocados, diced
- Shredded Cheddar cheese or crumbled cotija cheese
- Crispy tortilla strips or crushed tortilla chips

1. Rinse quinoa in fine-mesh strainer under cold running water. Place in medium saucepan. Add 1½ cups water, 3 cloves garlic, chili powder, 1 teaspoon salt, 1 teaspoon cumin and oregano. Bring to a boil over medium-high heat. Reduce heat to low. Cover and simmer 15 minutes or until quinoa is tender and most water is absorbed.
2. Meanwhile, heat 1 teaspoon oil in large skillet over medium-high heat. Add cauliflower and ½ teaspoon salt; cook and stir 10 minutes or until tender and browned. Add quinoa to cauliflower; cook and stir until well blended.
3. Heat 1 teaspoon oil in small skillet over medium heat. Add pepitas; cook and stir 3 to 5 minutes or until pepitas begin to pop and are lightly browned. Remove from heat. Season with remaining ¼ teaspoon salt.
4. For dressing, whisk remaining ¼ cup olive oil, ¼ teaspoon cumin and lime juice in medium bowl. Season with salt and pepper.
5. Arrange lettuce on large serving platter. Top with quinoa mixture, tomatoes, avocado, cheese, tortilla strips and pepitas. Serve with dressing.

Garbage Salad

Makes 4 to 6 servings

Dressing

- ⅓ cup red wine vinegar
- 2 cloves garlic, minced
- 2 teaspoons sugar
- 1 teaspoon Italian seasoning
- ¼ teaspoon salt
- ¼ teaspoon black pepper
- ⅓ cup vegetable or canola oil

Salad

- 1 package (5 ounces) mixed spring greens
- 5 romaine lettuce leaves, chopped
- 1 small cucumber, diced
- 2 small plum tomatoes, diced
- ½ red onion, thinly sliced
- ¼ cup pitted kalamata olives
- 4 radishes, thinly sliced
- 4 ounces thinly sliced Genoa salami, cut into ¼-inch strips
- 4 ounces provolone cheese, cut into ¼-inch strips
- ¼ cup grated Parmesan cheese

1. For dressing, whisk vinegar, garlic, sugar, Italian seasoning, salt and pepper in small bowl until blended. Slowly whisk in oil in thin, steady stream until well blended.
2. For salad, combine spring mix, romaine, cucumber, tomatoes, onion, olives and radishes in large bowl. Add half of dressing; toss gently to coat. Top with salami and provolone; sprinkle with Parmesan. Serve with remaining dressing.

Chicken and Apple Salad

Makes 4 servings

Dressing

- 5 tablespoons thawed frozen apple juice concentrate
- ¼ cup white balsamic vinegar
- 1 tablespoon lemon juice
- 1 tablespoon sugar
- 1 clove garlic, minced
- ½ teaspoon salt
- ½ teaspoon onion powder
- ¼ teaspoon ground ginger
- ¼ cup extra virgin olive oil

Salad

- 12 cups mixed greens such as chopped romaine lettuce and spring greens
- 12 ounces thinly sliced cooked chicken
- 2 tomatoes, cut into wedges
- 1 package (about 3 ounces) dried apple chips
- ½ red onion, thinly sliced
- ½ cup crumbled gorgonzola or blue cheese
- ½ cup pecans, toasted*

**To toast pecans, cook in medium skillet over medium heat 3 to 4 minutes or until lightly browned and fragrant, stirring frequently. Cool before using.*

1 For dressing, whisk apple juice concentrate, vinegar, lemon juice, sugar, garlic, salt, onion powder and ginger in small bowl until blended. Slowly whisk in oil until well blended.

2 For salad, divide greens among four serving bowls. Top with chicken, tomatoes, apple chips, onion, cheese and pecans.

3 Drizzle dressing over each salad.

Green Goddess Cobb Salad

Makes 4 servings

Pickled Onions

- 1 cup thinly sliced red onion
- ½ cup white wine vinegar
- ¼ cup water
- 2 teaspoons sugar
- 1 teaspoon salt

Dressing

- 1 cup mayonnaise
- 1 cup fresh parsley leaves
- 1 cup baby arugula
- ¼ cup extra virgin olive oil
- 3 tablespoons lemon juice
- 3 tablespoons minced fresh chives
- 2 tablespoons fresh tarragon leaves
- 1 clove garlic, minced
- 1 teaspoon Dijon mustard
- ½ teaspoon salt
- ⅛ teaspoon black pepper

Salad

- 4 cups Italian salad blend (romaine and radicchio)
- 2 cups chopped stemmed kale
- 2 cups baby arugula
- 2 avocados, halved and sliced
- 2 tomatoes, cut into wedges
- 2 cups grilled or roasted chicken breast strips
- 1 cup chopped crisp-cooked bacon
- 4 hard-cooked eggs (page 38), peeled and cut in half lengthwise

1 For pickled onions, combine onion, vinegar, ¼ cup water, sugar and 1 teaspoon salt in large glass jar. Seal jar; shake well. Refrigerate at least 1 hour or up to 1 week.

2 For dressing, combine mayonnaise, parsley, 1 cup arugula, oil, lemon juice, chives, tarragon, garlic, mustard, ½ teaspoon salt and pepper in blender or food processor; blend until smooth, stopping to scrape down side once or twice. Transfer to jar; refrigerate until ready to use. Just before serving, thin dressing with 1 to 2 tablespoons water, if necessary, to reach desired consistency.

3 For salad, combine salad blend, kale, 2 cups arugula and pickled onions in large bowl; divide among four serving bowls. Top each salad with avocados, tomatoes, chicken, bacon and two egg halves. Top with ¼ cup dressing; toss to coat.

Taco Salad Supreme

Makes 4 servings

Chili

- 1 pound ground beef
- 1 medium onion, chopped
- 1 stalk celery, chopped
- 2 fresh tomatoes, chopped
- 1 jalapeño pepper, minced
- 1½ teaspoons chili powder
- 1 teaspoon salt
- 1 teaspoon ground cumin
- ½ teaspoon black pepper
- 1 can (15 ounces) tomato sauce
- 1 can (about 15 ounces) kidney beans, rinsed and drained
- 1 can (about 15 ounces) pinto beans, rinsed and drained
- 1 cup water

Salad

- 8 cups chopped romaine lettuce (large pieces)
- 2 cups diced fresh tomatoes
- 48 small round tortilla chips
- 1 cup salsa
- ½ cup sour cream
- ½ cup (2 ounces) shredded Cheddar cheese

1. For chili, combine beef, onion and celery in large saucepan; cook over medium-high heat 6 to 8 minutes or until beef is no longer pink, stirring to break up meat. Drain fat.
2. Add chopped tomatoes, jalapeño, chili powder, salt, cumin and black pepper; cook and stir 1 minute. Stir in tomato sauce, beans and water; bring to a boil. Reduce heat to medium-low; cook 1 hour or until most of liquid is absorbed.
3. For each salad, combine 2 cups lettuce and ½ cup diced tomatoes in serving bowl. Top with 12 tortilla chips, ¾ cup chili, ¼ cup salsa and 2 tablespoons sour cream. Sprinkle with 2 tablespoons cheese. (Reserve remaining chili for another use.)

Superfood Kale Salad

Makes 4 servings

Maple-Roasted Carrots

- 8 carrots, trimmed
- 2 tablespoons olive oil
- 2 tablespoons maple syrup
- ½ teaspoon salt
- ⅛ teaspoon black pepper
- Dash ground red pepper

Maple-Lemon Vinaigrette

- ¼ cup extra virgin olive oil
- 3 tablespoons lemon juice
- 2 tablespoons maple syrup
- ¾ teaspoon grated lemon peel
- ½ teaspoon salt
- ⅛ teaspoon black pepper

Salad

- 4 cups chopped kale
- 2 cups chopped mixed greens
- 1 cup dried cranberries
- 1 cup slivered almonds, toasted*
- 1 cup shredded Parmesan cheese

**To toast almonds, cook in medium skillet over medium heat 3 to 4 minutes or until lightly browned and fragrant, stirring frequently. Cool before using.*

1. Preheat oven to 400°F. Line baking sheet with parchment paper.
2. Place carrots on prepared baking sheet. Whisk 2 tablespoons oil, 2 tablespoons maple syrup, ½ teaspoon salt, ⅛ teaspoon black pepper and red pepper in small bowl until well blended. Brush some of oil mixture over carrots. Roast 30 minutes or until carrots are tender, brushing with oil mixture and shaking baking sheet every 10 minutes. Cut carrots crosswise into ¼-inch slices when cool enough to handle.
3. Meanwhile for vinaigrette, whisk ¼ cup oil, lemon juice, 2 tablespoons maple syrup, lemon peel, ½ teaspoon salt and ⅛ teaspoon black pepper in small bowl until well blended.
4. Combine kale, greens, cranberries, almonds and cheese in large bowl. Add carrots. Pour vinaigrette over salad; toss to coat.

Crunchy Thai Salad

Makes 6 servings

Cilantro-Lime Dressing

- 1 cup loosely packed fresh cilantro leaves
- ½ cup vegetable oil
- ¼ cup chopped red bell pepper
- 2 tablespoons honey
- 2 tablespoons white vinegar
- 2 tablespoons lime juice
- 2 teaspoons Dijon mustard
- 2 teaspoons minced fresh ginger
- 1 teaspoon toasted sesame oil
- 1 teaspoon salt
- ¼ teaspoon black pepper

Thai Peanut Dressing

- ¼ cup creamy peanut butter
- 2 tablespoons hot water
- 2 tablespoons seasoned rice vinegar
- 2 tablespoons vegetable oil
- 2 tablespoons honey
- 2 tablespoons packed brown sugar
- 4 teaspoons soy sauce
- 1½ teaspoons salt
- ¼ teaspoon ground red pepper

Salad

- Vegetable oil for frying
- 2 bundles cellophane (bean thread) noodles (about 2 ounces)
- ½ (12-ounce) package wonton wrappers, cut into ½-inch strips
- 1 small head napa cabbage, cored and cut into ¼-inch strips
- 1 small head red cabbage, cut into wedges, cored and cut into ¼-inch strips
- 1 cup shredded carrots
- 1 bunch green onions, thinly sliced
- 1 seedless cucumber, peeled and julienned
- 2 cups shelled edamame (thawed if frozen)
- 1½ cups dry roasted peanuts
- ½ cup chopped fresh cilantro
- 2 cups chopped cooked chicken
- 2 avocados, diced

1 For cilantro dressing, combine 1 cup cilantro, ½ cup vegetable oil, bell pepper, 2 tablespoons honey, vinegar, lime juice, mustard, ginger, sesame oil, 1 teaspoon salt and black pepper in blender; blend until smooth.

2 For peanut dressing, whisk peanut butter, hot water, rice vinegar, 2 tablespoons vegetable oil, 2 tablespoons honey, brown sugar, 4 teaspoons soy sauce, 1½ teaspoons salt and ground red pepper in small bowl until well blended.

3 Heat 2 inches of oil in large saucepan over medium-high heat to 375°F. Fry cellophane noodles 5 seconds or until puffed, turning once. Drain on paper towel-lined plate. Use same oil to fry wonton strips in batches 1 to 2 minutes or until lightly browned, stirring occasionally to brown all sides. Drain on paper towel-lined plate.

4 Combine cabbages, carrots, green onions, cucumber, edamame, peanuts and ½ cup chopped cilantro in large bowl. Add cilantro dressing; toss to coat. Add chicken and avocado; stir gently to coat. Divide salad among serving plates; top with fried cellophane noodles and fried wontons. Drizzle with peanut dressing.

Autumn Harvest Salad

Makes 6 servings

Dressing

- ½ cup extra virgin olive oil
- 3 tablespoons balsamic vinegar
- 1 clove garlic, minced
- 1 teaspoon honey
- 1 teaspoon Dijon mustard
- ½ teaspoon dried oregano
- ½ teaspoon salt
- ⅛ teaspoon black pepper

Salad

- 1 loaf (12 to 16 ounces) artisan pecan raisin bread
- 4 tablespoons (½ stick) butter, melted
- 6 tablespoons coarse sugar (such as demerara, turbinado or organic cane sugar)
- 6 cups packed spring greens
- 2 Granny Smith apples, thinly sliced
- 1 package (12 to 16 ounces) grilled chicken breast strips
- ¾ cup crumbled blue cheese
- ¾ cup dried cranberries
- ¾ cup walnuts

1. For dressing, whisk oil, vinegar, garlic, honey, mustard, oregano, salt and pepper in medium bowl until well blended. Refrigerate until ready to use.
2. Preheat oven to 350°F. Line baking sheet with parchment paper. Cut bread into thin (¼-inch) slices; place in single layer on prepared baking sheet. Brush one side of each slice with melted butter; sprinkle each slice with ½ teaspoon sugar. Bake 10 minutes. Turn slices; brush with butter and sprinkle with ½ teaspoon sugar. Bake 10 minutes. Cool completely on baking sheet.
3. For each salad, place 1 cup greens on serving plate. Top with apple slices, chicken strips, cheese, cranberries and walnuts. Break two toast slices into pieces and sprinkle over salad. Drizzle with dressing.

Strawberry Chicken Salad

Makes 4 servings

Glazed Walnuts

- 2 tablespoons butter
- 6 tablespoons sugar
- 1 tablespoon honey
- ½ teaspoon salt
- ⅛ teaspoon ground red pepper
- 1 cup walnuts

Dressing

- 1 cup fresh strawberries, hulled
- ½ cup vegetable oil
- 6 tablespoons white wine vinegar
- 3 tablespoons sugar
- 3 tablespoons honey
- 2 tablespoons balsamic vinegar
- 2 teaspoons Dijon mustard
- ½ teaspoon dried oregano
- ¼ teaspoon salt

Salad

- 4 cups chopped romaine lettuce
- 4 cups coarsely chopped fresh spinach
- 1 cup sliced fresh strawberries
- ½ cup crumbled feta cheese
- 12 ounces grilled chicken breast strips *or* 2 cups warm chicken slices (about half of a rotisserie chicken)

1. For walnuts, preheat oven to 350°F. Line baking sheet with foil; spray with nonstick cooking spray.
2. Melt butter in medium skillet over medium-high heat. Stir in 6 tablespoons sugar, 1 tablespoon honey, ½ teaspoon salt and red pepper until well blended. Add walnuts; cook 3 minutes or until nuts are glazed and begin to brown, stirring occasionally. Spread in single layer on prepared baking sheet. Bake 7 minutes or until nuts are lightly browned and fragrant. Cool completely on baking sheet. Break into individual nuts.
3. For dressing, combine whole strawberries, oil, white wine vinegar, 3 tablespoons sugar, 3 tablespoons honey, balsamic vinegar, mustard, oregano and ¼ teaspoon salt in blender or food processor; blend 30 seconds or until smooth.
4. For each salad, combine 1 cup romaine and 1 cup spinach on serving plate; top with ¼ cup sliced strawberries, ¼ cup glazed walnuts and 2 tablespoons cheese. Top with chicken; drizzle with 2 tablespoons dressing.

Shrimp and Spinach Salad

Makes 4 servings

Dressing

- 4 slices bacon
- ¼ cup red wine vinegar
- ½ teaspoon cornstarch
- ¼ cup extra virgin olive oil
- ¼ cup sugar
- ¼ teaspoon salt
- ¼ teaspoon black pepper
- ¼ teaspoon liquid smoke

Shrimp

- 2 teaspoons black pepper
- 1 teaspoon salt
- 1 teaspoon garlic powder
- ½ teaspoon sugar
- ½ teaspoon onion powder
- ½ teaspoon ground sage
- ½ teaspoon paprika
- 20 to 24 large raw shrimp, peeled and deveined
- 2 tablespoons olive oil

Salad

- 8 cups packed torn stemmed spinach
- 1 tomato, diced
- ½ red onion, thinly sliced
- ½ cup sliced roasted red peppers

1. For dressing, cook bacon in large skillet over medium heat until crisp. Remove bacon with slotted spoon; drain on paper towel-lined plate. Crumble bacon; set aside.
2. Heat skillet with drippings over medium heat. Stir vinegar into cornstarch in small bowl until smooth. Whisk cornstarch mixture into drippings in skillet; cook 1 to 2 minutes or until slightly thickened, whisking constantly. Remove from heat; pour into small bowl or glass measuring cup. Whisk in ¼ cup oil, ¼ cup sugar, ¼ teaspoon salt, ¼ teaspoon black pepper and liquid smoke until well blended. Wipe out skillet with paper towel.
3. For shrimp, combine 2 teaspoons black pepper, 1 teaspoon salt, garlic powder, ½ teaspoon sugar, onion powder, sage and paprika in medium bowl; mix well. Add shrimp; toss to coat.
4. Heat 2 tablespoons oil in same skillet over medium-high heat. Add shrimp; cook 2 to 3 minutes per side or until shrimp are pink and opaque.
5. For salad, combine spinach, tomato, onion and roasted peppers in large bowl. Add two thirds of dressing; toss to coat. Top with shrimp and crumbled bacon; serve with remaining dressing.

Pecan-Crusted Chicken Salad

Makes 4 servings

Chicken

- ½ cup all-purpose flour
- ½ cup milk
- 1 egg
- ⅔ cup corn flake crumbs
- ⅔ cup finely chopped pecans
- ¾ teaspoon salt
- 4 boneless skinless chicken breasts (about 6 ounces each)

Dressing

- ⅓ cup balsamic vinegar
- 1 tablespoon Dijon mustard
- 1 tablespoon sugar
- 1 teaspoon minced garlic
- ½ teaspoon salt
- ⅔ cup vegetable or canola oil

Salad

- 8 cups mixed spring greens
- 2 cans (11 ounces each) mandarin oranges, drained
- 1 cup sliced celery
- ¾ cup dried cranberries
- ½ cup glazed pecans*
- ½ cup crumbled blue cheese

***Glazed or candied pecans or walnuts may found in the produce section of the supermarket with other salad toppings, or they may be found in the snack aisle.**

1. Preheat oven to 400°F. Line baking sheet with foil; spray with nonstick cooking spray.
2. Place flour in shallow dish. Beat milk and egg in another shallow dish. Combine corn flake crumbs, chopped pecans and ¾ teaspoon salt in third shallow dish. Dip both sides of chicken in flour, then in egg mixture, letting excess drip back into dish. Roll in crumb mixture to coat completely, pressing crumbs into chicken to adhere. Place on prepared baking sheet.
3. Bake 20 minutes or until chicken is cooked through (165°F). Cool completely before slicing. (Chicken can be prepared several hours in advance and refrigerated.)
4. Meanwhile for dressing, combine vinegar, mustard, sugar, garlic and ½ teaspoon salt in medium bowl; mix well. Slowly whisk in oil until well blended.

5 For salad, combine mixed greens, mandarin oranges, celery, cranberries, glazed pecans and cheese in large bowl. Add two thirds of dressing; toss gently to coat. Divide salad among four plates. Cut chicken breasts diagonally into ½-inch slices; arrange over salads. Serve with remaining dressing.

BBQ Chicken Salad

Makes 4 servings

Dressing

- ¾ cup mayonnaise
- ⅓ cup buttermilk
- ¼ cup sour cream
- 1 tablespoon white wine vinegar
- 1 teaspoon sugar
- ¼ teaspoon salt
- ¼ teaspoon garlic powder
- ¼ teaspoon onion powder
- ¼ teaspoon dried parsley flakes
- ¼ teaspoon dried dill weed
- ¼ teaspoon black pepper

Salad

- 1 package (12 to 16 ounces) grilled chicken breast strips
- ½ cup barbecue sauce
- 4 cups chopped romaine lettuce
- 4 cups chopped iceberg lettuce
- 2 medium tomatoes, seeded and chopped
- ¾ cup canned or thawed frozen corn, drained
- ¾ cup diced jicama
- ¾ cup (3 ounces) shredded Monterey Jack cheese
- ¼ cup chopped fresh cilantro
- 2 green onions, sliced
- 1 cup crispy tortilla strips

1. For dressing, whisk mayonnaise, buttermilk, sour cream, vinegar, sugar, salt, garlic powder, onion powder, parsley flakes, dill weed and pepper in medium bowl until well blended. Cover and refrigerate until ready to serve.
2. For salad, cut chicken strips into ½-inch pieces; place in medium bowl. Add barbecue sauce; stir to coat.
3. Combine lettuce, tomatoes, corn, jicama, cheese and cilantro in large bowl. Add two thirds of dressing; toss to coat. Add remaining dressing, if necessary. Divide salad among four plates; top with chicken, green onions and tortilla strips.

Chicken Waldorf Salad

Makes 4 servings

Dressing

- ⅓ cup balsamic vinegar
- 2 tablespoons Dijon mustard
- 2 teaspoons minced garlic
- ½ teaspoon salt
- ¼ teaspoon black pepper
- ⅔ cup extra virgin olive oil

Salad

- 8 cups mixed greens
- 1 large Granny Smith apple, cut into ½-inch pieces
- ⅔ cup diced celery
- ⅔ cup halved red grapes
- 1 package (12 to 16 ounces) grilled chicken breast strips
- ½ cup candied walnuts*
- ½ cup crumbled blue cheese

**Candied or glazed walnuts may found in the produce section of the supermarket with other salad toppings, or they may be found in the snack aisle.*

1. For dressing, whisk vinegar, mustard, garlic, salt and pepper in medium bowl. Slowly whisk in oil until well blended.
2. For salad, combine mixed greens, apple, celery and grapes in large bowl. Add half of dressing; toss to coat. Top with chicken, walnuts and cheese; drizzle with additional dressing.

Steakhouse Chopped Salad

Makes 8 to 10 servings

Dressing

- Italian Dressing Seasoning (recipe follows) *or* 1 package (about 2 tablespoons) Italian salad dressing mix
- ⅓ cup white balsamic vinegar
- ¼ cup Dijon mustard
- ⅔ cup extra virgin olive oil

Salad

- 1 medium head iceberg lettuce, chopped
- 1 medium head romaine lettuce, chopped
- 1 can (about 14 ounces) hearts of palm or artichoke hearts, quartered lengthwise then sliced crosswise
- 1 large avocado, diced
- 1½ cups crumbled blue cheese
- 2 hard-cooked eggs (page 38), peeled and chopped
- 1 ripe tomato, chopped
- ½ small red onion, finely chopped
- 1 package (12 ounces) bacon, crisp-cooked and crumbled

1 For dressing, prepare Italian Dressing Seasoning. Whisk vinegar, mustard and seasoning mix in small bowl. Slowly whisk in oil until well blended. Set aside until ready to use. (Dressing can be made up to 1 week in advance; refrigerate in jar with tight-fitting lid.)

2 For salad, combine iceberg lettuce, romaine, hearts of palm, avocado, cheese, eggs, tomato, onion and bacon in large bowl. Add dressing; toss gently to coat.

Italian Dressing Seasoning

Makes about 2½ tablespoons

- 1½ teaspoons salt
- 1½ teaspoons dried oregano
- ¾ teaspoon sugar
- ¾ teaspoon onion powder
- ¾ teaspoon dried parsley flakes
- ½ teaspoon garlic powder
- ¼ teaspoon dried basil
- ¼ teaspoon black pepper
- ⅛ teaspoon dried thyme
- ⅛ teaspoon celery salt

Combine all ingredients in small bowl; mix well.

Tuna Salad Niçoise

Makes 6 servings

Herb Vinaigrette

- ¼ cup white wine vinegar
- ¼ cup red wine vinegar
- ¼ cup chopped fresh basil
- 2 tablespoons chopped fresh chives
- 1 tablespoon Dijon mustard
- 2 cloves garlic, minced
- ½ teaspoon sugar
- ½ teaspoon salt
- ½ teaspoon black pepper
- 1 cup extra virgin olive oil

Salad

- 1 pound tuna steaks*
- 1½ pounds red potatoes, cubed
- 2 cups trimmed and halved green beans
- 8 cups mixed greens or chopped romaine lettuce
- 3 hard-cooked eggs (page 38), peeled and cut into wedges
- ½ cup pitted kalamata olives
- 4 medium tomatoes, cut into wedges

**Or substitute 2 cans (6 ounces each) tuna, drained and flaked and skip steps 2 and 3.*

1. For vinaigrette, combine vinegars, basil, chives, mustard, garlic, sugar, salt and pepper in food processor or blender; process 30 seconds or until smooth. With motor running, slowly add oil; process until smooth. Pour dressing into jar; refrigerate until ready to use.
2. For salad, place tuna in baking dish. Pour ¼ cup dressing over tuna; turn to coat. Marinate in refrigerator 30 minutes.
3. Prepare grill for direct cooking over medium heat or preheat broiler. Remove tuna from marinade; discard marinade. Grill or broil tuna 4 minutes per side or until desired doneness. Remove to cutting board; let stand 5 minutes. Cut into thin slices.
4. Bring large saucepan of salted water to a boil over medium-high heat. Add potatoes; cook 5 minutes. Add beans; cook 5 minutes or until potatoes are tender and beans are crisp-tender. Drain and return to saucepan. Add ¼ cup dressing; stir to coat.
5. Divide greens among serving plates; top with potatoes and green beans. Arrange eggs, olives, tomatoes and tuna on top. Serve with remaining dressing.

Pasta Salads

Salsa Pasta Salad

Makes 6 servings

- 1 package (12 ounces) uncooked tricolor rotini pasta
- 1¼ cups thick and chunky salsa
- ¾ cup drained canned corn or thawed frozen corn
- ¾ cup canned black beans, rinsed and drained
- 2 green onions, finely chopped
- ⅓ cup chopped fresh cilantro
- ¼ cup mayonnaise
- 1 jalapeño pepper, seeded and finely chopped
- ¼ teaspoon salt

1. Cook pasta in large saucepan of salted boiling water according to package directions for al dente. Drain and rinse under cold water until cool.
2. Combine salsa, corn, beans, green onions, cilantro, mayonnaise, jalapeño and salt in large bowl; mix well. Add pasta; stir to coat. Cover and refrigerate at least 1 hour before serving.

Broccoli Carrot Pasta Salad

Makes 8 servings

- 8 ounces uncooked rotini pasta
- 4 cups broccoli florets
- 2 cups carrot slices
- 1½ cups chopped tomatoes
- ½ cup chopped green onions
- 1 cup mayonnaise
- 2 tablespoons white wine vinegar
- 1 tablespoon extra virgin olive oil
- 1 tablespoon minced fresh basil *or* 1 teaspoon dried basil
- 2 teaspoons minced fresh oregano *or* ½ teaspoon dried oregano
- 1 clove garlic, minced
- 1 teaspoon sugar
- 1 teaspoon dry mustard
- ¼ teaspoon salt
- ¼ teaspoon black pepper
- ¼ cup grated Romano cheese

1. Cook pasta in large saucepan of salted boiling water according to package directions for al dente, adding broccoli and carrots during last 4 minutes of cooking. Drain and run under cold water until cool. Place in large bowl; stir in tomatoes and green onions.
2. Combine combine mayonnaise, vinegar, oil, basil, oregano, garlic, sugar, mustard, salt and pepper in small bowl. Pour over pasta mixture; mix well. Add cheese; stir until blended. Cover and refrigerate at least 3 hours or overnight to allow flavors to blend.

Ham and Pea Macaroni Salad

Makes 6 servings

- 1 cup uncooked elbow macaroni
- 1 cup frozen green peas
- 6 tablespoons mayonnaise
- ¼ cup plain yogurt or sour cream
- 1 tablespoon dill or sweet pickle relish
- 1 teaspoon dried dill weed
- 1 teaspoon yellow mustard
- ¼ teaspoon salt
- 1 cup chopped green bell pepper
- ½ cup thinly sliced celery
- 4 ounces ham, cubed
- ½ cup (2 ounces) shredded Cheddar cheese, divided

1. Cook pasta in large saucepan of salted boiling water according to package directions for al dente, adding peas during last 1 minute of cooking. Drain and rinse under cold water until cool.
2. Meanwhile, combine mayonnaise, yogurt, pickle relish, dill weed, mustard and salt in large bowl; stir until well blended. Add pasta, peas, bell pepper, celery and ham.
3. Stir in 6 tablespoons cheese; sprinkle top with remaining 2 tablespoons cheese. Serve immediately.

Lentil and Orzo Pasta Salad

Makes 4 servings

- ½ cup dried lentils, rinsed and sorted
- 4 ounces uncooked orzo pasta
- 1½ cups quartered cherry or grape tomatoes
- ¾ cup finely chopped celery
- ½ cup chopped red onion
- 16 pitted kalamata olives, coarsely chopped
- ¼ cup cider vinegar
- 1 tablespoon extra virgin olive oil
- 1 clove garlic, minced
- 1 teaspoon dried basil
- 1 teaspoon dried oregano
- ½ teaspoon salt
- ⅛ teaspoon red pepper flakes
- 4 ounces crumbled feta cheese with sun-dried tomatoes and basil

1. Bring large saucepan of salted water to a boil over high heat. Add lentils; cook 12 minutes.
2. Add orzo; cook 10 minutes or just until lentils and orzo are tender. Drain and rinse under cold water to cool completely.
3. Meanwhile, combine tomatoes, celery, onion, olives, vinegar, oil, garlic, basil, oregano, salt and red pepper flakes in large bowl; mix well.
4. Add lentil mixture to tomato mixture; toss gently to blend. Add cheese; toss gently. Let stand 15 minutes before serving.

Rigatoni Salad

Makes 8 servings

- 12 ounces rigatoni pasta, cooked and drained
- 1 to 2 cups chopped greens, such as arugula, frisée or any crisp lettuce
- 1 package (10 ounces) frozen snow peas or sugar snap peas, thawed
- 8 ounces cherry tomatoes, halved
- 1 medium red or yellow bell pepper, cut into thin strips
- ½ red onion, cut into thin strips
- ⅓ cup sliced black olives
- ⅓ to ½ cup Italian dressing, store-bought or homemade (page 182)
- Shredded Parmesan cheese (optional)

1. Cook pasta in large saucepan of salted boiling water according to package directions for al dente. Drain and place in large bowl.
2. Add greens, peas, tomatoes, bell pepper, onion and olives; mix well. Add dressing; toss to coat. Sprinkle with cheese, if desired.

Mediterranean Pasta Salad

Makes 6 servings

- 12 ounces uncooked rotini pasta
- 1 cup cut fresh green beans (1-inch pieces)
- 1 cup Italian dressing, store-bought or homemade (page 182)
- 1 can (about 6 ounces) tuna packed in water, drained
- 3 hard-cooked eggs (page 38), peeled and cut into wedges
- ¼ cup pitted black olives

1. Cook pasta in large saucepan of salted boiling water according to package directions for al dente, adding green beans during last 4 minutes of cooking. Drain and rinse under cold water until cool. Place in large bowl.
2. Reserve ¼ cup salad dressing; stir remaining dressing into pasta.
3. Add tuna, egg and olives to pasta and green beans. Drizzle with reserved vinaigrette. Serve cold or at room temperature.

Colorful Pasta Salad

Makes 8 servings

- 4 ounces uncooked spinach rotini or fusilli
- ½ cup finely chopped carrot
- ½ cup chopped celery
- ½ cup chopped red bell pepper
- 2 green onions, sliced
- 3 tablespoons balsamic vinegar
- 2 tablespoons mayonnaise
- 2 teaspoons whole grain mustard
- ½ teaspoon black pepper
- ¼ teaspoon Italian seasoning
- Leaf lettuce

1. Cook pasta in large saucepan of salted boiling water according to directions for al dente. Drain and rinse under cold water until cool.
2. Combine pasta, carrot, celery, bell pepper and green onions in medium bowl.
3. Whisk vinegar, mayonnaise, mustard, black pepper and Italian seasoning in small bowl until blended. Pour over salad; toss to coat evenly. Cover and refrigerate up to 8 hours.
4. Serve salad on lettuce-lined plates, if desired.

Green Bean, Walnut and Blue Cheese Pasta Salad

Makes 6 servings

- 2 cups uncooked gemelli pasta
- 2 cups trimmed halved green beans
- 3 tablespoons extra virgin olive oil
- 2 tablespoons white wine vinegar
- 1 tablespoon chopped fresh thyme *or* 1 teaspoon dried thyme
- 1 tablespoon Dijon mustard
- 1 tablespoon lemon juice
- 1 teaspoon honey
- ¼ teaspoon salt
- ¼ teaspoon black pepper
- ½ cup chopped walnuts, toasted*
- ½ cup crumbled blue cheese

**To toast walnuts, spread in single layer in medium. Cook and stir over medium heat 3 to 4 minutes or until nuts are lightly browned. Cool before using.*

1 Cook pasta in large saucepan of salted boiling water according to package directions for al dente, adding green beans during last 4 minutes of cooking. Drain; place in large bowl.

2 Meanwhile for dressing, whisk oil, vinegar, thyme, mustard, lemon juice, honey, salt and pepper in medium bowl until smooth and well blended.

3 Pour dressing over pasta and green beans; toss to coat evenly. Stir in walnuts and cheese. Serve warm or cover and refrigerate until ready to serve.**

***If serving cold, stir walnuts into salad just before serving.*

Chicken and Gnocchi Caesar Salad

Makes 4 servings

- 4 boneless skinless chicken breasts (about 6 ounces each)
- Salt and black pepper
- 6 ounces uncooked gnocchi or medium shell pasta
- 1 package (9 ounces) frozen artichoke hearts, thawed
- 1½ cups cherry tomatoes, quartered
- ¼ cup plus 2 tablespoons plain yogurt or sour cream
- 2 tablespoons mayonnaise
- 2 tablespoons grated Romano cheese
- 1 tablespoon sherry or red wine vinegar
- 1 clove garlic, minced
- ½ teaspoon anchovy paste
- ½ teaspoon Dijon mustard
- ½ teaspoon white pepper
- 1 small head romaine lettuce, torn into 1-inch pieces
- 1 cup croutons, store-bought or homemade (page 18)

1. Season chicken all over with salt and pepper. Grill or broil chicken 8 minutes or until cooked through (165°F); set aside.
2. Cook pasta in large saucepan of salted boiling water according to package directions for al dente. Drain and rinse under cold water until cool. Combine pasta, artichoke hearts and tomatoes in large bowl.
3. Combine yogurt, mayonnaise, cheese, sherry, garlic, anchovy paste, mustard and pepper in small bowl; whisk until smooth. Add to pasta mixture; toss to coat evenly.
4. Arrange lettuce on serving plates. Spoon pasta mixture over lettuce. Thinly slice chicken and place on top of salad. Sprinkle with croutons.

Greek Pasta Salad

Makes 8 servings

- 1 package (16 ounces) uncooked rotini pasta
- 1½ cups diced cucumber
- 2 medium tomatoes, diced
- 1 green bell pepper, diced
- ½ cup (2 ounces) finely crumbled feta cheese
- 12 pitted kalamata olives, sliced into thirds
- ¼ cup chopped fresh dill
- Juice of ½ lemon
- ¼ teaspoon salt
- ⅛ teaspoon black pepper

1. Cook pasta in large saucepan of salted boiling water according to package directions for al dente. Drain and rinse under cold water until cool. Place in large bowl.
2. Stir cucumber, tomatoes, bell pepper, feta, olives and dill into pasta. Add lemon juice, salt and pepper; mix well. Cover and refrigerate until ready to serve.

Thai-Style Warm Noodle Salad

Makes 4 servings

- 8 ounces uncooked angel hair pasta
- ½ cup creamy or chunky peanut butter
- ¼ cup soy sauce
- ¼ to ½ teaspoon red pepper flakes
- 2 green onions, thinly sliced
- 1 carrot, shredded

1 Cook pasta in large saucepan of salted boiling water according to package directions for al dente. Drain, reserving 5 tablespoons pasta cooking water.

2 Meanwhile, whisk peanut butter, soy sauce and red pepper flakes in large bowl until smooth. Whisk hot pasta water into peanut butter mixture until smooth. Add pasta to sauce; toss to coat. Stir in green onions and carrot. Serve warm or at room temperature.

Rotini Salad with Artichokes and Sun-Dried Tomatoes

Makes 8 servings

- ½ cup balsamic or red wine vinegar
- 3 tablespoons extra virgin olive oil
- 2 cloves garlic, minced
- 8 ounces uncooked rigatoni or penne pasta
- 1 can (14 ounces) artichoke hearts in water, drained and cut into quarters
- ½ cup oil-packed sun-dried tomatoes, drained and chopped
- ¼ cup chopped fresh basil
- ½ cup chopped or sliced black olives
- 4 ounces crumbled feta cheese with sun-dried tomatoes and basil
- 3 cups fresh baby spinach, stemmed and torn
- Salt and black pepper
- ¼ cup toasted* pine nuts (optional)

**To toast pine nuts, cook in medium skillet over medium heat 3 to 4 minutes or until lightly browned and fragrant, stirring frequently. Cool before using.*

1. Whisk vinegar, oil and garlic in small bowl until well blended.
2. Cook pasta in large saucepan of salted boiling water according to package directions for al dente. Drain; cool completely.
3. Combine pasta, artichokes, tomatoes, basil, olives and cheese in large bowl; mix well. Add spinach and dressing; toss to coat. Season to taste with salt and pepper. Top with pine nuts, if desired.

Pasta Salad Niçoise

Makes 4 servings

- 2 cups uncooked medium shell pasta
- ½ cup Italian dressing, store-bought or homemade (page 182)
- ½ cup chopped fresh basil
- 2 cloves garlic, minced
- ¼ teaspoon salt
- ¼ teaspoon black pepper
- ¼ teaspoon red pepper flakes
- 2 cans (6 ounces each) tuna, packed in water, drained and flaked
- 1 cup diced tomato
- ½ cup thinly sliced red onion
- ¼ cup chopped black olives
- Assorted chopped lettuce (optional)

1. Cook pasta in large saucepan of salted boiling water according to package directions for al dente. Drain; cool completely.
2. Whisk dressing, basil, garlic, salt, black pepper and red pepper in small bowl.
3. Combine pasta, tuna, tomato, onion and olives in large bowl. Add dressing; toss to coat. Refrigerate until ready to serve. Serve on lettuce, if desired.

Apple and Broccoli Pasta Salad

Makes 6 servings

- 8 ounces uncooked cavatappi pasta
- 2 cups broccoli florets
- 1 medium Red or Golden Delicious apple, chopped
- ⅔ cup shredded carrots
- ⅓ cup plain yogurt or sour cream
- ⅓ cup apple juice
- 3 tablespoons cider vinegar
- 1 tablespoon extra virgin olive oil
- 1 tablespoon Dijon mustard
- 1 teaspoon honey
- ½ teaspoon dried thyme

1 Cook pasta in large saucepan of salted boiling water according to package directions for al dente, adding broccoli during last 2 minutes of cooking. Drain and rinse under cold water until cool. Place in medium bowl; stir in apple and carrots.

2 Whisk yogurt, apple juice, vinegar, oil, mustard, honey and thyme in small bowl until smooth and well blended. Pour over pasta mixture; toss to coat. Refrigerate until ready to serve.

Vegetable Salads

Broccoli and Cauliflower Salad

Makes 8 servings

- 1 package (12 ounces) bacon, chopped
- 2 cups mayonnaise
- ¼ cup sugar
- ¼ cup white or cider vinegar
- 4 cups chopped broccoli
- 4 cups coarsely chopped cauliflower
- 1½ cups (6 ounces) shredded Cheddar cheese
- 1 cup chopped red onion
- 1 cup dried cranberries or raisins
- ½ cup sunflower seeds (optional)
- Salt and black pepper

1. Cook bacon in large skillet over medium heat until crisp, stirring frequently. Remove from skillet with slotted spoon; drain on paper towel-lined plate.
2. Whisk mayonnaise, sugar and vinegar in large bowl. Stir in broccoli, cauliflower, cheese, onion and cranberries; mix well. Fold in bacon and sunflower seeds, if desired. Season with salt and pepper.
3. Serve immediately or cover and refrigerate until ready to serve.

Pepita Lime Cabbage Slaw

Makes 8 servings

- ½ red onion, thinly sliced
- 3 tablespoons cider vinegar
- 1 teaspoon sugar
- 2½ teaspoons salt, divided
- ½ teaspoon ground cumin
- ¼ teaspoon onion powder
- ⅛ teaspoon ground coriander
- ⅛ teaspoon celery seed
- 1 tablespoon plus 2 teaspoons extra virgin olive oil
- ½ cup pepitas
- ⅛ teaspoon black pepper
- 4 cups thinly sliced green cabbage (about ⅛ head)
- 4 cups thinly sliced red cabbage (about ½ small head)
- 3 tablespoons chopped fresh cilantro
- 2 tablespoons lime juice

1. Place onion in large bowl. Add vinegar, sugar and 1 teaspoon salt; mix well. Let stand at least 20 minutes. Combine cumin, onion powder, coriander, celery seed and 1 teaspoon salt in small bowl.
2. Meanwhile, heat 2 teaspoons oil in small skillet over medium heat. Add pepitas; cook and stir 5 minutes or until pepitas are lightly browned and beginning to pop. Season with remaining ½ teaspoon salt and pepper. Remove to plate; cool completely.
3. Add green cabbage, red cabbage and cilantro to onion in large bowl. Drizzle with remaining 1 tablespoon oil and lime juice and sprinkle with seasoning mix. Mix thoroughly with hands, squeezing to blend evenly. Sprinkle with pepitas; toss gently to blend.

Warm Potato Salad

Makes 6 servings

- **2 pounds fingerling potatoes**
- **2¾ teaspoons salt, divided**
- **3 slices thick-cut bacon, chopped**
- **1 small onion, diced**
- **2 tablespoons olive oil**
- **¼ cup cider vinegar**
- **2 tablespoons capers, drained**
- **1 tablespoon Dijon mustard**
- **¼ teaspoon black pepper**
- **⅓ cup chopped fresh parsley**

1. Place potatoes in large saucepan; add cold water to cover by 2 inches and stir in 2 teaspoons salt. Bring to a boil over high heat. Reduce heat to medium; cook 10 to 12 minutes or just until potatoes are fork-tender.
2. Drain potatoes; let stand until cool enough to handle. Meanwhile, dry out saucepan with paper towels. Add bacon to saucepan; cook and stir until crisp. Remove bacon to paper towel-lined plate with slotted spoon; drain off all but 1 tablespoon drippings.
3. Add onion and oil to saucepan; cook 10 minutes or until onion begins to turn golden, stirring occasionally. Cut potatoes crosswise into ½-inch slices.
4. Add vinegar, capers, mustard, remaining ½ teaspoon salt and pepper to saucepan; mix well. Remove from heat; stir in potatoes. Add parsley and bacon; stir gently to coat. Serve warm.

Cauliflower Chopped Salad

Makes 8 servings

Cauliflower

- ½ cup red wine vinegar
- ¼ cup extra virgin olive oil
- 1 teaspoon salt
- 1 teaspoon honey
- 1 teaspoon Dijon mustard
- ½ teaspoon dried oregano
- 1 clove garlic, minced
- ¼ teaspoon black pepper
- 2 cups small cauliflower florets (½ inch)

Salad

- 1 head iceberg lettuce, chopped
- 1 container (4 ounces) crumbled blue cheese
- 1 pint grape tomatoes, halved *or* 1 cup finely chopped tomatoes
- ½ cup finely chopped red onion
- 2 green onions, finely chopped
- 1 avocado, diced

1. For cauliflower, whisk vinegar, oil, salt, honey, mustard, oregano, garlic and pepper in medium bowl. Add cauliflower; stir to coat. Cover and refrigerate several hours or overnight.

2. For salad, combine lettuce, blue cheese, tomatoes, red onion and green onions in large bowl; toss to coat. Remove cauliflower from marinade using slotted spoon; place on salad. Whisk marinade; pour over salad and toss to coat. Top with avocado; mix gently.

Edamame Peanut Slaw

Makes 6 to 8 servings

- 4 cups thinly sliced green cabbage
- 3 cups thinly sliced red cabbage (about ½ of small head)
- 1 red bell pepper, thinly sliced
- 1 cup thawed frozen shelled edamame
- 3 green onions, thinly sliced
- 1 carrot, shredded or julienned
- Juice of 1 lime
- 2 tablespoons unseasoned rice vinegar
- 1 tablespoon toasted sesame oil
- 2 teaspoons salt
- 1 teaspoon sugar
- 1 teaspoon minced fresh ginger
- 1 cup roasted peanuts

1. Combine cabbage, bell pepper, edamame, green onions and carrot in large bowl; mix well.
2. Whisk lime juice, vinegar, oil, salt, sugar and ginger in small bowl until salt and sugar are dissolved. Pour dressing over salad; mix well. Stir in peanuts just before serving.

Note

This slaw can be made a day or two day ahead of time. Adjust the salt, lime juice and vinegar before serving. For crunchy peanuts, stir them in just before serving. They will also be fine if you stir them in early and let them sit. Their texture will be more crisp-tender than crisp, similar to the edamame.

Zucchini Chickpea Salad

Makes 4 to 6 servings

- 3 medium zucchini (about 6 ounces each)
- ½ teaspoon salt
- 5 tablespoons white vinegar
- 1 clove garlic, minced
- ¼ teaspoon dried thyme
- ½ cup extra virgin olive oil
- 1 cup drained canned chickpeas
- ½ cup sliced pitted black olives
- 3 green onions, minced
- 1 ripe avocado, cut into ½-inch cubes
- ⅓ cup crumbled feta cheese
- 1 canned chipotle pepper in adobo sauce, seeded and minced
- Boston lettuce leaves and sliced fresh tomatoes (optional)

1. Cut zucchini lengthwise into halves; cut halves crosswise into ¼-inch-thick slices. Place slices in medium bowl; sprinkle with salt. Toss to mix. Spread zucchini on several layers of paper towels. Let stand at room temperature 30 minutes to drain.
2. Combine vinegar, garlic and thyme in large bowl. Slowly whisk in oil until well blended. Pat zucchini dry; add to dressing. Add chickpeas, olives and onions; toss lightly to coat. Cover and refrigerate at least 30 minutes or up to 4 hours, stirring occasionally.
3. Add avocado, cheese and chipotle pepper to salad just before serving. Stir gently to mix. If desired, line shallow bowls or small plates with lettuce leaves and tomato slices; top with salad.

Cabbage and Red Potato Salad

Makes 4 servings

- ½ cup finely chopped cilantro
- 2 tablespoons lime juice
- 2 tablespoons extra virgin olive oil
- 2 teaspoons honey
- ½ teaspoon ground cumin
- 2¼ teaspoons salt, divided
- 1 pound baby red potatoes (about 4 potatoes), quartered
- 2 cups sliced napa cabbage
- 2 cups sliced red cabbage
- ½ cup sliced green onions
- 2 tablespoons sunflower kernels

1. Whisk cilantro, lime juice, oil, honey, cumin and ¼ teaspoon salt in small bowl until smooth and well blended. Let stand 30 minutes to allow flavors to blend.
2. Place potatoes in large saucepan; add cold water to cover by 2 inches and stir in remaining 2 teaspoons salt. Bring to a boil over high heat. Reduce heat to medium; cook 10 to 12 minutes or just until potatoes are fork-tender. Drain and place in large bowl; cool completely.
3. Add napa cabbage, red cabbage and green onions to potatoes. Add dressing; toss to coat evenly. Sprinkle with sunflower kernels just before serving.

Carrot Cranberry Slaw

Makes about 3 cups

- 2 cups shredded carrots*
- 1 package (3 ounces) ramen noodles, crumbled**
- ¼ cup chopped walnuts
- ¼ cup dried cranberries
- 2 tablespoons chopped green onion
- 2 tablespoons mayonnaise
- 1 tablespoon packed brown sugar
- 1 teaspoon lime juice
- ½ teaspoon honey
- Salt and black pepper

**For convenience, purchase packaged shredded carrots; 2 cups is about half of a 10-ounce package.*

***Use any flavor; discard seasoning packet.*

1. Combine carrots, noodles, walnuts, cranberries and green onion in medium bowl.
2. Combine mayonnaise, brown sugar, lime juice and honey in small bowl. Pour over salad; stir gently to coat. Season to taste with salt and pepper. Cover and refrigerate until ready to serve.

Cauliflower Caprese Salad

Makes 8 servings

- 1 head cauliflower, cut into florets and thinly sliced
- ¾ cup balsamic vinegar
- ½ cup extra virgin olive oil
- 1 teaspoon salt
- 1 teaspoon sugar
- 1 clove garlic, minced
- 1 teaspoon Italian seasoning
- 1 container (8 ounces) pearl-shaped fresh mozzarella cheese *or* 1 (8-ounce) ball fresh mozzarella, sliced or chopped
- 1 pint grape tomatoes, halved *or* 2 cups chopped fresh tomatoes
- ¼ cup shredded fresh basil

1. Place cauliflower in large resealable food storage bag or large bowl. Add vinegar, oil, salt, sugar, garlic and Italian seasoning. Seal bag; shake to coat. Marinate in refrigerator 8 hours or overnight.
2. Pour cauliflower and marinade into large bowl. Stir in cheese, tomatoes and basil.

Note

Turn leftovers into a pasta entrée. Cook pasta (any shape) according to package directions. Drain and immediately toss with leftover caprese salad. Serve warm or at room temperature.

Green Bean and Egg Salad

Makes 4 to 6 servings

- 1 pound green beans, trimmed and cut into 2-inch pieces
- 3 hard-cooked eggs (page 38), peeled and chopped
- 2 stalks celery, cut into slices
- ½ cup Cheddar cheese cubes (¼-inch cubes)
- ¼ cup chopped red onion
- ⅓ cup mayonnaise
- 2 teaspoons cider vinegar
- 1½ teaspoons sugar
- ½ teaspoon salt
- ½ teaspoon celery seed
- ⅛ teaspoon black pepper

1. Bring large saucepan of salted water to a boil. Add beans; cook 4 minutes or until crisp-tender. Drain and rinse under cold water to stop cooking. Place in large bowl. Stir in eggs, celery, cheese and onion.
2. Combine mayonnaise, vinegar, sugar, salt, celery seed and pepper in small bowl; mix well. Pour over salad; gently stir until coated. Cover and refrigerate at least 1 hour before serving.

Grain & Bean Salads

Quinoa and Mango Salad

Makes 6 servings

- 1 cup uncooked quinoa
- 2 cups water
- 2 cups cubed peeled mangoes (about 2 large mangoes)
- ½ cup sliced green onions
- ½ cup dried cranberries
- 2 tablespoons chopped fresh parsley
- ¼ cup extra virgin olive oil
- 1 tablespoon plus 1½ teaspoons white wine vinegar
- 1 teaspoon Dijon mustard
- ½ teaspoon salt
- ⅛ teaspoon black pepper

1. Place quinoa in fine-mesh strainer; rinse well under cold running water. Combine quinoa and 2 cups water in medium saucepan; bring to a boil over high heat. Reduce heat to low. Cover and simmer 15 minutes until quinoa is tender and water is absorbed. Place in large bowl; cover and refrigerate at least 1 hour or until cool.
2. Add mangoes, green onions, cranberries and parsley to quinoa; mix well.
3. Combine oil, vinegar, mustard, salt and pepper in small bowl; whisk until blended. Pour over quinoa mixture; mix until well blended.

Chickpea Chopped Salad

Makes 8 servings

- ½ cup plus 2 tablespoons extra virgin olive oil, divided
- 1 cup chopped walnuts
- 1 teaspoon salt, divided
- 4 cups chopped green cabbage
- 2 cups chopped red cabbage
- 1 cup drained canned chickpeas
- 1 green bell pepper, chopped
- ½ cup chopped fresh parsley
- 1 carrot, shredded
- ½ cup red wine vinegar
- 1½ tablespoons honey
- 2 cloves garlic, minced
- ½ teaspoon Italian seasoning
- ¼ teaspoon black pepper
- ⅛ teaspoon red pepper flakes
- 1 avocado, diced

1. Heat 2 tablespoons oil in small skillet over medium-high heat. Add walnuts; cook and stir 4 to 5 minutes or until walnuts are fragrant and lightly toasted. Stir in ½ teaspoon salt. Transfer to paper towel-lined plate; cool completely.
2. Combine green cabbage, red cabbage, chickpeas, bell pepper, parsley and carrot in large bowl.
3. For dressing, whisk vinegar, honey, garlic, seasoning, remaining ½ teaspoon salt, black pepper and red pepper flakes in medium bowl until well blended. Slowly whisk in remaining ½ cup oil until well blended. Add to salad; toss to coat. Stir in avocado and walnuts.

Farro, Grape and Roasted Carrot Bowl

Makes 4 to 6 servings

- 1 pound carrots, peeled, trimmed and halved lengthwise
- 4 tablespoons extra virgin olive oil, divided
- 1 teaspoon salt, divided
- ½ teaspoon ground cumin
- ¼ teaspoon ground coriander
- ⅛ teaspoon ground nutmeg
- 1 package (2¼ ounces) slivered almonds
- 2 cups water
- 1 cup uncooked farro, rinsed under cold water
- 2 tablespoons balsamic vinegar
- 1 cup halved red grapes
- ¼ cup minced red onion
- Salt and black pepper
- 4 cups mixed spring greens

1. Preheat oven to 375°F. Place carrots on baking sheet. Drizzle with 1 tablespoon oil. Combine ½ teaspoon salt, cumin, coriander and nutmeg in small bowl; sprinkle over carrots. Toss to coat carrots with oil and spices. Arrange cut sides down in single layer.
2. Roast 30 minutes or until carrots are browned and tender, turning once. Place almonds on small baking sheet; bake about 5 minutes or until toasted, stirring frequently.
3. Meanwhile, bring 2 cups water and remaining ½ teaspoon salt to a boil in medium saucepan. Stir in farro. Reduce heat to medium-low; cover and simmer 25 minutes or until tender. Drain and place farro in large bowl.
4. Whisk remaining 3 tablespoons oil into vinegar in small bowl; pour over farro. Stir in grapes and onion; season to taste with additional salt and pepper. Cut carrots into 1-inch pieces; add to farro mixture. Place greens in bowls; top with farro salad and almonds.

Texas Caviar

Makes about 9 cups

- 1 tablespoon vegetable oil
- 1 cup fresh corn (from 2 to 3 ears)
- 2 cans (about 15 ounces) black-eyed peas, rinsed and drained
- 1 can (about 15 ounces) black beans
- 1 cup halved grape tomatoes
- 1 bell pepper (red, orange, yellow or green), finely chopped
- ½ cup finely chopped red onion
- 1 jalapeño pepper, seeded and minced
- 2 green onions, minced
- ¼ cup chopped fresh cilantro
- 2 tablespoons red wine vinegar
- 1 tablespoon plus 1 teaspoon lime juice, divided
- 1 teaspoon salt
- 1 teaspoon sugar
- ½ teaspoon ground cumin
- ½ teaspoon dried oregano
- 2 cloves garlic, minced
- ¼ cup extra virgin olive oil

1. Heat vegetable oil in large skillet over high heat. Add corn; cook and stir about 3 minutes or until corn is beginning to brown in spots. Place in large bowl. Add beans, tomatoes, bell pepper, onion, jalapeño, green onions and cilantro.
2. Combine vinegar, 1 tablespoon lime juice, salt, sugar, cumin, oregano and garlic in small bowl. Slowly whisk in oil until well blended. Pour over vegetables; stir to coat.
3. Refrigerate at least 2 hours or overnight. Just before serving, stir in remaining 1 teaspoon lime juice. Taste and season with additional salt, if desired.

Note

Serve Texas Caviar as a dip for a crowd with corn chips or tortilla chips. It also makes a great packable lunch or side dish.

Farro, Chickpea and Spinach Salad

Makes 6 servings

- 1 cup uncooked pearled farro
- 3 cups baby spinach, stemmed
- 1 medium cucumber, chopped
- 1 can (about 15 ounces) chickpeas, rinsed and drained
- ¾ cup pitted kalamata olives
- ¼ cup extra virgin olive oil
- 3 tablespoons white or golden balsamic vinegar *or* 3 tablespoons cider vinegar mixed with ½ teaspoon sugar
- 1 teaspoon chopped fresh rosemary
- 1 clove garlic, minced
- 1 teaspoon salt
- ⅛ to ¼ teaspoon red pepper flakes (optional)
- ½ cup (2 ounces) crumbled goat or feta cheese

1. Bring large saucepan of water to a boil over high heat. Stir in farro. Reduce heat to medium-low; cover and simmer 25 minutes or until tender. Drain and rinse under cold water until cool.
2. Meanwhile, combine spinach, cucumber, chickpeas, olives, oil, vinegar, rosemary, garlic, salt and red pepper flakes, if desired, in large bowl. Stir in farro until well blended. Add cheese; stir gently.

Grilled Chicken and Three Bean Salad

Makes 4 to 6 servings

- 2 boneless skinless chicken breasts (about 6 ounces each)
- Salt and black pepper
- 2 cups cut green beans (1-inch pieces)
- ¾ cup canned kidney beans
- ¾ cup canned pinto beans
- 2 cups mixed baby greens
- ¼ cup minced fresh chives
- ¼ cup sour cream
- 2 tablespoons buttermilk or milk
- 1 tablespoon Dijon mustard
- 1 teaspoon minced fresh dill
- ¼ teaspoon salt
- ¼ teaspoon black pepper
- Pinch ground cumin

1. Season chicken all over with salt and pepper. Grill or broil until chicken is cooked through (165°F). Let stand until cool enough to handle. Cut into cubes.
2. Bring large saucepan of salted boiling water to a boil. Add green beans; cook 4 minutes or until crisp-tender. Drain and rinse under cold water until cool.
3. Combine chicken, green beans, kidney beans, pinto beans and greens in large salad bowl.
4. Whisk chives, sour cream, buttermilk, mustard, dill, ¼ teaspoon salt, ¼ teaspoon pepper and cumin in small bowl. Pour over chicken mixture; toss gently to coat.

Pesto Farro and Asparagus Salad

Makes 6 servings

- 1 cup uncooked pearled farro
- 1 cup frozen peas
- 1 pound asparagus, trimmed and cut into 1-inch pieces
- 2 cups fresh packed basil leaves
- ½ cup packed fresh Italian parsley
- ¼ cup toasted walnuts
- 2 cloves garlic
- ½ cup extra virgin olive oil
- ½ cup grated Parmesan cheese
- Salt and black pepper
- ½ cup (2 ounces) crumbled feta cheese

1 Bring large saucepan of water to a boil over high heat. Stir in farro. Reduce heat to medium-low; cover and simmer 25 minutes or until tender, adding peas during last 5 minutes of cooking time and asparagus during last 2 minutes of cooking time. Drain and place in large bowl.

2 Meanwhile, place basil, parsley, walnuts and garlic in food processor. Pulse until coarsely chopped. With motor running, slowly add oil. Add Parmesan cheese; pulse to combine. Season with salt and pepper.

3 Add pesto to farro; stir to coat. Add feta cheese; stir until combined. Season to taste with additional salt and pepper, if desired.

Fiesta Corn Salad

Makes 4 to 6 servings

- 5 ears fresh corn
- 1 cup plain yogurt or sour cream
- 3 tablespoons minced onion
- 1½ tablespoons lime juice
- 1 clove garlic, minced
- 1 teaspoon ground cumin
- 1 teaspoon chili powder
- ¼ teaspoon salt
- 1½ cups shredded red cabbage
- 1 large tomato, chopped
- 1 green bell pepper, seeded and chopped
- 1 cup (4 ounces) shredded Cheddar cheese
- 5 slices bacon, crisp-cooked and crumbled (optional)
- 1 cup coarsely crushed tortilla chips

1. Bring large saucepan of water to a boil over high heat. Remove husks and silk from corn. Place corn in boiling water. Cover and cook 6 minutes or until tender; drain. Cool completely.
2. For dressing, whisk yogurt, onion, lime juice, garlic, cumin, chili powder and salt in small bowl until well blended.
3. Cut corn from cob using sharp knife; place corn in large bowl. Add cabbage, tomato and bell pepper. Pour dressing over salad; mix lightly. Cover and refrigerate until ready to serve. Stir in cheese and bacon, if desired, just before serving. Spoon salad into large bowl; sprinkle with chips.

Greek Chickpea Salad

Makes 4 servings

- 4 cups packed stemmed baby spinach
- 1 can (about 15 ounces) chickpeas, rinsed and drained
- 1 large shallot, thinly sliced
- ¼ cup pitted kalamata olives, sliced
- ¼ cup crumbled feta cheese
- ¼ cup plain Greek yogurt
- 1 tablespoon white wine vinegar
- 1 tablespoon extra virgin olive oil
- 1 clove garlic, minced
- ¼ teaspoon salt
- ¼ teaspoon black pepper

1. Combine spinach, chickpeas, shallot, olives and cheese in large bowl; toss gently.
2. Whisk yogurt, vinegar, oil, garlic, salt and pepper in small bowl until well blended. Add to salad just before serving; toss gently.

White Bean and Orzo Salad

Makes 6 servings

- ¾ cup (6 ounces) uncooked orzo pasta
- 1 can (about 15 ounces) navy beans, rinsed and drained
- 1 cup packed spinach leaves, coarsely chopped
- ½ cup chopped roasted red peppers
- 3 tablespoons capers, rinsed and drained
- 3 tablespoons chopped fresh basil
- 3 tablespoons Italian dressing, store-bought or homemade (page 182)
- ¼ cup crumbled feta cheese

1 Cook orzo in large saucepan of salted boiling water according to package directions for al dente. Drain and place in large bowl.

2 Add beans, spinach, peppers, capers, basil and dressing to pasta; gently stir until combined. Stir in cheese.

Barley and Bean Salad

Makes 4 to 6 servings

- ⅔ cup uncooked pearl barley
- 3 cups cut asparagus (1-inch pieces)
- 2 cans (about 15 ounces each) red kidney beans, rinsed and drained
- 2 tablespoons chopped fresh mint
- ¼ cup lemon juice
- ¼ cup Italian dressing, store-bought or homemade (page 182)
- ¼ teaspoon black pepper
- ¼ cup sunflower seeds

1 Cook barley in large saucepan of salted boiling water according to package directions. Add asparagus during last 5 minutes of cooking. Drain barley and asparagus; place in large bowl. Refrigerate at least 2 hours.

2 Stir beans and mint into barley mixture. Whisk lemon juice, salad dressing and pepper in small bowl until well blended. Add to salad; toss to coat. Sprinkle with sunflower seeds.

Deli Salads

Chickpea Salad

Makes 4 servings

- 1 can (about 15 ounces) chickpeas, rinsed and drained
- 1 stalk celery, chopped
- 1 dill pickle, chopped (about ½ cup)
- ¼ cup finely chopped red or yellow onion
- ⅓ cup mayonnaise
- 1 teaspoon lemon juice
- ¼ teaspoon salt (optional)
- Black pepper
- Whole grain bread
- Lettuce and tomato slices (optional)

1. Place chickpeas in medium bowl. Coarsely mash with potato masher, leaving some beans whole.
2. Add celery, pickle and onion; stir to blend. Add mayonnaise and lemon juice; mix well. Taste and add ¼ teaspoon salt or more, if desired. Season with pepper; mix well. Serve on bread with lettuce and tomato, if desired.

Almond Chicken Salad

Makes 4 servings

- ¼ cup mayonnaise
- ¼ cup plain Greek yogurt or sour cream
- 2 tablespoons cider vinegar
- 1 tablespoon honey
- 1 teaspoon salt
- ½ teaspoon black pepper
- ⅛ teaspoon garlic powder
- 2 cups chopped cooked chicken
- ¾ cup halved red grapes
- 1 large stalk celery, chopped
- ⅓ cup sliced almonds
- Leaf lettuce
- 1 tomato, thinly sliced
- 8 slices sesame semolina or country Italian bread

1. Whisk mayonnaise, yogurt, vinegar, honey, salt, pepper and garlic powder in small bowl until well blended.
2. Combine chicken, grapes and celery in medium bowl. Add dressing; toss gently to coat. Cover and refrigerate several hours or overnight. Stir in almonds just before serving.
3. Place lettuce and tomato slices on four bread slices; top with chicken salad and remaining bread slices. Serve immediately.

Green Bean Potato Salad

Makes 6 servings

- ½ cup Pickled Red Onions (recipe follows)
- 2 pounds unpeeled red potatoes, thinly sliced and cut in half
- 1 cup green beans, cut into 1-inch pieces
- 2 tablespoons plain Greek yogurt or sour cream
- 2 tablespoons white wine vinegar
- 2 tablespoons extra virgin olive oil
- 1 tablespoon spicy mustard
- 1 teaspoon salt

1. Prepare Pickled Red Onions.
2. Bring large saucepan of salted water to a boil. Add potatoes; cook 4 minutes. Add green beans; cook 2 minutes or until vegetables are fork-tender. Drain and transfer to large bowl. Stir in onions.
3. Combine yogurt, vinegar, oil, mustard and salt in small bowl well blended. Pour over vegetables; stir gently to coat. Cover and refrigerate at least 1 hour to allow flavors to blend.

Pickled Red Onions

Makes about 1 cup

- 1 small red onion, thinly sliced
- ½ cup white wine vinegar
- 2 tablespoons water
- 1 teaspoon sugar
- 1 teaspoon salt

Combine all ingredients in large jar or food storage container. Seal jar; shake well. Refrigerate at least 1 hour or up to 1 week.

Cantaloupe Chicken Salad

Makes 2 servings

- 1 large cantaloupe
- 1 package (3 ounces) ramen noodles, crumbled, divided*
- 1 cup diced cooked chicken
- ½ cup red grapes, halved
- ¼ cup chopped green bell pepper
- ¼ cup diced red onion
- 2 tablespoons vegetable oil
- 2 tablespoons sugar
- 1 tablespoon white vinegar

***Use any flavor; discard seasoning packet.**

1. Cut cantaloupe in half and remove seeds. Scoop out melon from each half, leaving ½-inch shell. Chop melon; measure ½ cup.
2. Combine ½ cup noodles, chicken, grapes, bell pepper, onion and ½ cup chopped melon in large bowl.
3. Whisk oil, sugar and vinegar in small bowl. Pour over salad; mix well.
4. Divide salad between cantaloupe halves. Sprinkle remaining noodles over top to serve.

Easy Caesar Tuna Salad

Makes 2 servings

1 can (6 ounces) solid white tuna packed in water, drained and flaked

2 tablespoons Caesar dressing, store-bought or homemade (page 185)

½ cup chopped celery

Salt and black pepper

Combine tuna, dressing and celery in medium bowl. Season with salt and pepper.

Tarragon Potato Salad

Makes 6 to 8 servings

- 6 medium red potatoes (about 1¾ pounds)
- 2½ teaspoons salt, divided
- 1 cup frozen peas, thawed
- ¾ cup chopped green bell pepper
- ¾ cup mayonnaise
- ¼ cup milk
- ¼ cup sliced green onions
- 2 tablespoons chopped fresh parsley
- 1 tablespoon lemon juice
- 2 teaspoons dried tarragon
- ¼ teaspoon black pepper
- Lettuce leaves (optional)

1. Place potatoes in large saucepan; cover with 2 inches of water and stir in 2 teaspoons salt. Bring to a boil over medium-high heat; boil 25 minutes or until tender. Drain potatoes. When cool enough to handle, slice potatoes.
2. Combine potatoes, peas and bell pepper in large bowl. Stir mayonnaise, milk, green onions, parsley, lemon juice, tarragon, remaining ½ teaspoon salt and black pepper in small bowl until well blended. Pour over potato mixture; gently stir to coat. Cover and refrigerate at least 4 hours.
3. Serve salad on lettuce-lined plates, if desired.

Colorful Coleslaw

Makes 4 to 6 servings

- **¼ head green cabbage, shredded or thinly sliced**
- **¼ head red cabbage, shredded or thinly sliced**
- **1 yellow or orange bell pepper, thinly sliced**
- **1 small jicama, peeled and julienned**
- **¼ cup thinly sliced green onions**
- **2 tablespoons chopped fresh cilantro**
- **¼ cup vegetable oil**
- **¼ cup lime juice**
- **1 teaspoon salt**
- **⅛ teaspoon black pepper**

1. Combine cabbage, bell pepper, jicama, green onions and cilantro in large bowl.
2. Whisk oil, lime juice, salt and black pepper in small bowl until well blended. Pour over vegetables; toss to coat. Cover; refrigerate 2 to 6 hours for flavors to blend.

Note

This coleslaw makes a great topping for tacos and sandwiches.

Cauliflower Picnic Salad

Makes 6 servings

- 1 teaspoon salt
- 1 head cauliflower, cut into 1-inch florets
- ¾ cup mayonnaise
- 1 tablespoon yellow mustard
- 2 tablespoons minced fresh parsley
- ⅓ cup chopped dill pickle
- ⅓ cup minced red onion
- 2 hard-cooked eggs (page 38), peeled and chopped
- Salt and black pepper (optional)

1 Fill large saucepan with 1 inch water. Bring to a simmer over medium-high heat; stir in 1 teaspoon salt. Add cauliflower; reduce heat to medium. Cover and cook 5 to 7 minutes or until cauliflower is fork-tender but not mushy. Drain and cool slightly.

2 Combine mayonnaise, mustard and parsley in large bowl; stir in pickle and onion. Gently fold in cauliflower and eggs. Season with salt and pepper, if desired.

Chicken Peanut Salad

Makes 6 servings

- ¾ cup mayonnaise
- 1 teaspoon ground cumin
- 1 teaspoon lemon juice
- ½ teaspoon onion powder
- ½ teaspoon salt
- ¼ teaspoon garlic powder
- ¼ teaspoon black pepper
- 3 cups diced cooked chicken
- 1 cup red grapes, cut into halves
- 1 cup diced jicama
- ½ cup chopped red bell pepper
- Leaf lettuce
- ½ cup salted peanuts, chopped

1. Combine mayonnaise, cumin, lemon juice, onion powder, salt, garlic powder and black pepper in medium bowl. Combine chicken, grapes, jicama and bell pepper in large bowl. Pour dressing over chicken mixture; stir well. Cover and refrigerate until cold.
2. Line plates with lettuce; spoon chicken salad over top. Sprinkle with peanuts.

Green Chile Potato Salad

Makes 6 servings

- 5 large red or white potatoes (about 2 pounds)
- 2½ teaspoons salt, divided
- 4 slices bacon, chopped
- ½ cup canned diced mild green chiles, drained
- ⅓ cup chopped fresh parsley
- ¼ cup finely chopped onion
- ⅓ cup vegetable oil
- 3 tablespoons white wine vinegar
- ¼ teaspoon black pepper
- ¼ teaspoon ground cumin
- 3 drops hot pepper sauce

1. Place potatoes in large saucepan; cover with 2 inches of water and stir in 2 teaspoons salt. Bring to a boil over high heat. Reduce heat to medium; simmer 25 minutes or until fork-tender. Drain and let stand until cool enough to handle.
2. Meanwhile, cook and stir bacon in medium skillet over medium-high heat until crisp. Drain bacon on paper towels; cool completely.
3. Cut potatoes into cubes; place in large bowl. Add bacon, chiles, parsley and onion; mix lightly.
4. Whisk oil, vinegar, remaining ½ teaspoon salt, black pepper, cumin and hot pepper sauce in small bowl until well blended. Pour over potato mixture; toss gently to coat. Cover and refrigerate 2 hours to allow flavors to blend.

Apple Walnut Tuna Salad

Makes 4 servings

- ½ cup mayonnaise
- 1 teaspoon lemon juice
- ½ teaspoon ground cumin
- ¼ teaspoon salt
- ¼ teaspoon sugar
- ¼ teaspoon onion powder
- ¼ teaspoon black pepper
- 1 can (about 12 ounces) tuna packed in water, drained and flaked
- 1 tart red apple, cored and chopped
- ½ cup chopped celery
- ⅓ cup chopped walnuts, toasted*
- ⅓ cup raisins
- Leaf lettuce
- ½ cup (2 ounces) shredded sharp Cheddar cheese

1 Whisk mayonnaise, lemon juice, cumin, salt, sugar, onion powder and pepper in small bowl until well blended.

2 Combine tuna, apple, celery, walnuts and raisins in large bowl. Add mayonnaise mixture; stir to coat. Cover and refrigerate at least 30 minutes.

3 Line four plates with lettuce; sprinkle with cheese. Spoon salad onto cheese.

**To toast walnuts, cook in medium skillet over medium heat 3 to 4 minutes or until lightly browned and fragrant, stirring frequently. Cool before using.*

Creamy Potato Salad

Makes 10 servings

- 3 pounds red potatoes, cut into 1-inch pieces
- 2 teaspoons salt
- 1 cup mayonnaise
- ½ cup Italian dressing, store-bought or homemade (page 182)
- 1 teaspoon Dijon mustard
- 1 teaspoon lemon juice
- ½ cup sliced green onions
- Salt and black pepper

1. Place potatoes in large saucepan; cover with 2 inches of water and stir in 2 teaspoons salt. Bring to a boil over high heat. Reduce heat to medium; simmer 10 minutes or until fork-tender. Drain and place in large bowl; cool completely.
2. Whisk mayonnaise, Italian dressing, mustard and lemon juice in small bowl. Pour over potatoes; stir until coated. Stir in green onions; season to taste with additional salt and pepper.

Curried Tuna Salad

Makes 4 servings

- 1 can (about 12 ounces) tuna packed in water, drained and flaked
- 3 tablespoons mayonnaise
- 2 tablespoons sour cream or plain yogurt
- 1 to 1½ tablespoons sugar
- 1 teaspoon curry powder
- ¼ teaspoon ground cumin
- 4 ounces sliced water chestnuts, drained and coarsely chopped
- ⅛ teaspoon ground red pepper
- Cinnamon-raisin bread, toasted (optional)

1. Combine tuna, mayonnaise, sour cream, sugar, curry powder and cumin in medium bowl; mix well. Add water chestnuts and red pepper; mix well.
2. Cover and refrigerate 15 minutes to allow flavors to blend. Serve on toast, if desired.

Egg Salad

Makes 4 servings

- 6 eggs
- 3 tablespoons mayonnaise
- ½ cup finely chopped celery
- 2 tablespoons chopped dill pickle or sweet pickle relish
- ⅛ to ¼ teaspoon salt
- Black pepper (optional)
- Whole wheat bread (optional)

1. Bring medium saucepan of water to a boil. Gently add eggs with slotted spoon. Reduce heat to maintain a simmer; cook 12 minutes. Meanwhile, fill medium bowl with cold water and ice cubes. Drain eggs and place in ice water; cool 10 minutes.
2. Peel and chop eggs; place in medium bowl (or place in medium bowl and mash with fork). Stir in mayonnaise, celery, pickle and salt. Season to taste with black pepper. Serve on bread, if desired.

Fruit Salads

Tomato Watermelon Salad

Makes 4 servings

Dressing

- ¼ cup extra virgin olive oil
- 2 tablespoons fresh lemon juice
- ½ teaspoon honey
- ½ teaspoon salt
- ⅛ teaspoon black pepper

Salad

- 2 large heirloom tomatoes (about 10 ounces each), cut into 6 slices each
- 2 cups cubed watermelon (about 12 ounces)
- ¼ cup thinly sliced red onion rings
- ¼ cup crumbled feta cheese
- Chopped fresh chervil or parsley (optional)

1. For dressing, whisk oil, lemon juice, honey, salt and pepper in small bowl until well blended.
2. For salad, arrange tomato slices on four plates. Top with watermelon and onion; sprinkle with cheese. Drizzle with dressing; garnish with chervil.

Fruit Salad with Creamy Banana Dressing

Makes 8 servings

- 2 cups fresh pineapple chunks
- 1 cup cantaloupe cubes
- 1 cup honeydew melon cubes
- 1 cup fresh blackberries
- 1 cup sliced fresh strawberries
- 1 cup red grapes
- 1 medium apple, diced
- 2 medium ripe bananas, sliced
- ½ cup vanilla Greek yogurt
- 2 tablespoons honey
- 1 tablespoon lemon juice
- ¼ teaspoon ground nutmeg

1. Combine pineapple, cantaloupe, honeydew, blackberries, strawberries, grapes and apple in large bowl; mix gently.
2. Combine bananas, yogurt, honey, lemon juice and nutmeg in blender or food processor; blend until smooth.
3. Pour dressing over fruit mixture; gently toss to coat. Serve immediately.

Crunchy Jicama, Radish and Melon Salad

Makes 8 servings

- 3 cups thinly cut jicama
- 3 cups watermelon cubes
- 2 cups cantaloupe cubes
- 1 cup sliced radishes
- 3 tablespoons chopped fresh cilantro
- 2 tablespoons extra virgin olive oil
- 2 tablespoons lime juice
- 1 tablespoon orange juice
- 1 tablespoon cider vinegar
- 1 tablespoon honey
- ½ teaspoon salt

1. Combine jicama, watermelon, cantaloupe and radishes in large bowl; gently mix.
2. Whisk cilantro, oil, lime juice, orange juice, vinegar, honey and salt in small bowl until smooth and well blended. Add to salad; gently toss to coat evenly. Serve immediately.

Spinach-Melon Salad

Makes 6 servings

- 6 cups packed stemmed baby spinach
- 3 cups mixed melon balls or cubes (cantaloupe, honeydew and/or watermelon)
- 1 cup zucchini ribbons*
- ½ cup sliced red bell pepper
- ¼ cup thinly sliced red onion
- ¼ cup red wine vinegar
- 2 tablespoons honey
- 2 teaspoons extra virgin olive oil
- 2 teaspoons lime juice
- 1 teaspoon poppy seeds
- 1 teaspoon dried mint

1 Combine spinach, melon, zucchini, bell pepper and onion in large bowl.

2 Whisk vinegar, honey, oil, lime juice, poppy seeds and mint in small bowl until well blended. Pour over salad; toss gently to coat.

**To make ribbons, thinly slice zucchini lengthwise with vegetable peeler or spiral cutter.*

Crunchy Orange Salad

Makes 4 servings

- ⅓ cup extra virgin olive oil
- 2 tablespoons cider vinegar
- 2 teaspoons honey
- 2 teaspoons dried tarragon
- ½ teaspoon dry mustard
- ¼ teaspoon salt
- ⅛ teaspoon black pepper
- 1 can (11 ounces) mandarin oranges, drained and 1 tablespoon juice reserved
- 4 cups chopped romaine lettuce
- 1 package (3 ounces) ramen noodles, lightly crumbled*
- ½ cup toasted** pecans, coarsely chopped
- ¼ cup chopped red onion

***Use any flavor; discard seasoning packet.**

****To toast pecans, cook in medium skillet over medium heat 3 to 4 minutes or until lightly browned and fragrant, stirring frequently. Cool before using.**

1. Whisk oil, vinegar, honey, tarragon, mustard, salt, pepper and reserved orange juice in large bowl.
2. Add lettuce, oranges, noodles, pecans and onion to dressing; toss to combine.

Cheesy Waldorf Salad

Makes 6 to 8 servings

- ⅓ cup mayonnaise
- 1 tablespoon honey
- 1 tablespoon cider vinegar
- 4 small *or* 3 large apples, cored and cut into ½-inch pieces (about 4 cups)
- 4 ounces provolone cheese, cubed
- 2 stalks celery, thinly sliced
- ½ cup walnuts or pecans, toasted* and chopped, divided
- Leaf lettuce

**To toast walnuts, spread in single layer in medium skillet. Cook and stir 1 to 2 minutes over medium heat until nuts are lightly browned. Cool completely.*

1 Combine mayonnaise, honey and vinegar in large bowl until blended. Add apples, cheese, celery and ¼ cup walnuts; stir to coat. (Salad may be refrigerated up to 8 hours at this point.)

2 Line individual salad plates with lettuce; top with salad. Sprinkle remaining ¼ cup walnuts over each serving.

Creamy Coconut-Lime Fruit Salad

Makes 6 to 8 servings

- ½ cup sour cream
- ½ cup unsweetened coconut milk
- 2 tablespoons lime juice
- 2 tablespoons packed brown sugar
- 2 seedless oranges, peeled and sectioned
- 2 Granny Smith apples, cored and chopped
- 2 ripe nectarines, pitted and sliced
- 1 ripe mango, peeled, pitted and diced
- 1 cup strawberry halves

1. Whisk sour cream, coconut milk, lime juice and brown sugar in small bowl until smooth.
2. Combine oranges, apples, nectarines, mango and strawberries in large bowl. Add sour cream mixture; stir to coat. Serve immediately or cover and refrigerate up to 4 hours.

Strawberry Salad

Makes 12 to 14 servings

- 2 packages (4-serving size each) strawberry-flavored gelatin
- 1 cup boiling water
- 2 packages (10 ounces each) frozen strawberries, thawed
- 1 can (20 ounces) crushed pineapple, drained
- 1 container (16 ounces) sour cream
- 1 container (8 ounces) thawed whipped topping
- Sliced fresh strawberries and fresh mint leaves (optional)

1. Combine gelatin and boiling water in large bowl; stir until dissolved. Add frozen strawberries and pineapple; mix well.
2. Pour half of gelatin mixture into medium glass serving bowl or 13×9-inch baking dish. Refrigerate until soft set.
3. Spread sour cream over gelatin in bowl. Pour remaining gelatin mixture over sour cream. Refrigerate until ready to serve. Spread whipped topping over gelatin; garnish with fresh strawberries and mint.

German Fruit Salad

Makes 8 servings

- **2 jars (16 ounces each) maraschino cherries, drained**
- **2 cans (11 ounces each) mandarin oranges, drained**
- **1 can (20 ounces) fruit cocktail, drained**
- **1 container (16 ounces) sour cream**
- **1 tablespoon mayonnaise**
- **½ cup chopped walnuts (optional)**
- **2 large red apples, cored and cut into bite-size pieces**
- **2 bananas, cut into bite-size pieces**

1. Combine cherries, oranges and fruit cocktail in large serving bowl.
2. Whisk sour cream and mayonnaise in medium bowl until well blended. Add to fruit mixture; stir gently to coat. Stir in walnuts, if desired. Cover and refrigerate 2 hours.
3. Stir in apples and bananas just before serving.

Fruit Salad with Strawberry Vinaigrette

Makes 6 servings

- 2 cups fresh strawberry slices, divided
- 3 tablespoons vegetable oil
- 2 tablespoons lime juice
- 2 tablespoons red wine vinegar
- 1 teaspoon sugar
- 1 bunch watercress, trimmed
- 1 avocado, sliced
- 2 cups cantaloupe balls or cubes

1. Combine 1 cup strawberries, oil, lime juice, vinegar and sugar in food processor; process until smooth. Strain mixture through fine-mesh sieve to remove seeds.
2. Arrange watercress on plates; top with avocado, cantaloupe and remaining 1 cup strawberries. Drizzle with vinaigrette.

Jalapeño Honey Fruit Salad

Makes 6 servings

- ⅓ cup orange juice
- 3 tablespoons lime juice
- 3 tablespoons minced fresh mint, basil or cilantro
- 2 jalapeño peppers, seeded and minced
- 1 tablespoon honey
- ½ small honeydew melon, cut into cubes
- 1 large ripe papaya, peeled, seeded, cubed
- 1 pint fresh strawberries, stemmed and halved
- 1 can (8 ounces) pineapple chunks, drained

1. Combine orange juice, lime juice, mint, jalapeño peppers and honey in small bowl.
2. Combine melon, papaya, strawberries and pineapple in large bowl. Pour orange juice mixture over fruit; toss gently until well blended.
3. Serve immediately or cover and refrigerate up to 3 hours.

Salad Dressings

Italian Dressing

Makes about ⅔ cup

- 3 tablespoons red wine vinegar
- 1 teaspoon minced garlic
- 1 teaspoon honey
- 1 teaspoon Dijon mustard
- ½ teaspoon salt
- ½ teaspoon onion powder
- ½ teaspoon dried basil
- ¼ teaspoon dried oregano
- ¼ cup vegetable oil
- ¼ cup extra virgin olive oil

Combine vinegar, garlic, honey, mustard, salt, onion powder, basil and oregano in medium bowl. Slowly whisk in oils until blended. Refrigerate in tightly-covered container until ready to use. Whisk before using.

Sesame Vinaigrette

Makes about ½ cup

- 3 tablespoons reduced-sodium soy sauce
- 1½ tablespoons toasted sesame oil
- 1 tablespoon water
- 1 tablespoon balsamic or red wine vinegar
- 2 teaspoons sugar
- 1 clove garlic, minced

Whisk all ingredients in small bowl until well blended. Refrigerate in tightly-covered container until ready to use. Whisk before using.

Balsamic Vinaigrette

Makes about ⅔ cup

- ¼ cup water
- ¼ cup balsamic vinegar
- 3 tablespoons extra virgin olive oil
- 2 tablespoons minced red onion
- 3 cloves garlic, minced
- ¾ teaspoon dried chervil
- ½ teaspoon celery seeds

Whisk all ingredients in small bowl until well blended. Refrigerate in tightly-covered container until ready to use. Whisk before using.

Creamy Blue Cheese Dressing

Makes about 1¼ cups

- ¾ cup mayonnaise
- ½ cup buttermilk
- ½ cup crumbled blue cheese
- 1 clove garlic, minced
- ½ teaspoon sugar
- ⅛ teaspoon onion powder
- ⅛ teaspoon salt
- ⅛ teaspoon black pepper

Combine all ingredients in food processor or blender; process until smooth. Refrigerate in tightly-covered container until ready to use. Whisk before using.

Pineapple Poppy Seed Dressing

Makes 1½ cups

- ¾ cup vegetable oil
- ⅓ cup pineapple juice
- ¼ cup diced canned pineapple
- 2 tablespoons cider vinegar
- ¼ small onion
- ½ teaspoon salt
- 2 teaspoons poppy seeds

Place oil, pineapple juice, pineapple, vinegar, onion and salt in food processor or blender; process to combine. Add poppy seeds; pulse until blended. Refrigerate in tightly-covered container until ready to use. Whisk before using.

Basil Vinaigrette

Makes about ½ cup

- 6 tablespoons extra virgin olive oil
- 3 tablespoons white wine vinegar
- 2 tablespoons minced fresh basil
- 2 teaspoons minced fresh chives
- 1 clove garlic, minced
- ¼ teaspoon black pepper
- ⅛ teaspoon salt

Whisk all ingredients in small bowl until well blended. Refrigerate in tightly-covered container until ready to use. Whisk before using.

Greek Vinaigrette

Makes 1½ cups

- ½ cup lemon juice
- ¼ red wine vinegar
- ¼ cup chopped fresh oregano
- 2 cloves garlic, minced
- 1 teaspoon salt
- ½ teaspoon black pepper
- ½ cup extra virgin olive oil

Whisk all ingredients in small bowl until well blended. Refrigerate in tightly-covered container until ready to use. Whisk before using.

Peanut Dressing

Makes about 2 cups

- ¾ cup creamy peanut butter
- ½ cup water
- 3 tablespoons rice vinegar
- 2 tablespoons soy sauce
- 2 tablespoons molasses
- 1 tablespoon anchovy paste
- 2 tablespoons chopped fresh cilantro
- 2 tablespoons chopped green onion

Whisk all ingredients in small bowl until well blended. Refrigerate in tightly-covered container until ready to use. Whisk before using.

Caesar Dressing

Makes 1 cup

- 2 tablespoons lemon juice
- 2 tablespoons sour cream
- 1 tablespoon red wine vinegar
- 2 anchovy fillets *or* 1 tablespoon anchovy paste
- 2 teaspoons Dijon mustard
- 2 cloves garlic
- ¾ cup olive oil
- ¼ cup grated Parmesan cheese

Combine lemon juice, sour cream, vinegar, anchovies, mustard and garlic in food processor. Process until combined. Slowly add olive oil while processing until thickened. Stir in cheese. Refrigerate in tightly-covered container until ready to use. Stir before using.

Creamy Avocado Dressing

Makes about 1 cup

- 2 ripe avocados, peeled and pitted
- Juice of 2 limes
- 2 tablespoons sour cream
- 2 tablespoons olive oil
- 1 teaspoon salt
- ½ teaspoon ground red pepper
- ½ teaspoon cumin

Combine all ingredients in food processor; process until well blended. Refrigerate in tightly-covered container until ready to use.

Honey Mustard Dressing

Makes 1 cup

- ¾ cup mayonnaise
- 2 tablespoons Dijon mustard
- 2 tablespoons honey
- 2 tablespoons rice wine vinegar
- 1 teaspoon soy sauce
- 1 teaspoon toasted sesame oil

Combine all ingredients in medium bowl. Refrigerate in tightly-covered container until ready to use. Stir before using.

Buttermilk Ranch Dressing

Makes 1¼ cups

¾ cup mayonnaise
½ cup buttermilk
2 tablespoons chopped fresh chives
1 tablespoon chopped fresh parsley or cilantro
1 clove garlic, minced
1 teaspoon salt
1 lemon juice or white wine vinegar
½ teaspoon sugar
½ teaspoon black pepper

Combine all ingredients in medium bowl. Refrigerate in tightly-covered container until ready to use. Stir before using.

Creamy Garlic Dressing

Makes 1 cup

½ cup mayonnaise
½ cup sour cream
Juice of 1 lemon
3 cloves garlic, minced
1 tablespoon red wine vinegar
Salt and black pepper

Combine all ingredients in medium bowl. Refrigerate in tightly-covered container until ready to use. Stir before using.

Fresh Herb Dressing

Makes about ¾ cup

½ cup red wine vinegar
¼ cup extra virgin olive oil
1 clove garlic, minced
1 tablespoon chopped fresh oregano
1 tablespoon chopped fresh parsley or marjoram
½ teaspoon sugar
¼ teaspoon salt
⅛ teaspoon black pepper

Whisk all ingredients in small bowl until well blended. Refrigerate in tightly-covered container until ready to use. Whisk before using.

Asian Dressing

Makes about 3 cups

- 1 large onion, sliced
- 1 cup water, divided
- ¼ cup soy sauce
- ¼ cup rice vinegar
- 1 tablespoon minced garlic
- 1 tablespoon minced fresh ginger
- 1 tablespoon toasted sesame oil
- 1 tablespoon lemon juice
- 1½ teaspoons sugar
- 1½ teaspoons black pepper
- 1½ teaspoons hot pepper sauce
- 2 tablespoons cornstarch

1. Preheat oven to 400°F. Spread onion on large baking sheet. Heat 15 minutes or until edges are dark brown.
2. Place onion in food processor; process until smooth. Pour into medium saucepan. Add ¾ cup water, soy sauce, rice vinegar, garlic, ginger, sesame oil, lemon juice, sugar, black pepper and hot pepper sauce; bring to a boil over medium-high heat.
3. Stir remaining ¼ cup water into cornstarch in small bowl until smooth. Gradually stir into saucepan; return to a boil. Reduce heat to low; simmer 2 to 3 minutes. Cool completely. Refrigerate in tightly-covered container until ready to use.

Stilton Salad Dressing

Makes about ⅔ cup

- ½ cup buttermilk
- ¼ cup sour cream
- 2 ounces Stilton cheese
- 2 tablespoons mayonnaise
- 1 teaspoon lemon juice
- 1 clove garlic, peeled
- ¼ teaspoon salt
- ⅛ teaspoon black pepper

Combine all ingredients in food processor or blender; process until smooth. Refrigerate in tightly-covered container until ready to use. Whisk before using.

Metric Conversion Chart

VOLUME MEASUREMENTS (dry)

1/8 teaspoon = 0.5 mL
1/4 teaspoon = 1 mL
1/2 teaspoon = 2 mL
3/4 teaspoon = 4 mL
1 teaspoon = 5 mL
1 tablespoon = 15 mL
2 tablespoons = 30 mL
1/4 cup = 60 mL
1/3 cup = 75 mL
1/2 cup = 125 mL
2/3 cup = 150 mL
3/4 cup = 175 mL
1 cup = 250 mL
2 cups = 1 pint = 500 mL
3 cups = 750 mL
4 cups = 1 quart = 1 L

VOLUME MEASUREMENTS (fluid)

1 fluid ounce (2 tablespoons) = 30 mL
4 fluid ounces (1/2 cup) = 125 mL
8 fluid ounces (1 cup) = 250 mL
12 fluid ounces (1 1/2 cups) = 375 mL
16 fluid ounces (2 cups) = 500 mL

WEIGHTS (mass)

1/2 ounce = 15 g
1 ounce = 30 g
3 ounces = 90 g
4 ounces = 120 g
8 ounces = 225 g
10 ounces = 285 g
12 ounces = 360 g
16 ounces = 1 pound = 450 g

DIMENSIONS

1/16 inch = 2 mm
1/8 inch = 3 mm
1/4 inch = 6 mm
1/2 inch = 1.5 cm
3/4 inch = 2 cm
1 inch = 2.5 cm

OVEN TEMPERATURES

250°F = 120°C
275°F = 140°C
300°F = 150°C
325°F = 160°C
350°F = 180°C
375°F = 190°C
400°F = 200°C
425°F = 220°C
450°F = 230°C

BAKING PAN SIZES

Utensil	Size in Inches/Quarts	Metric Volume	Size in Centimeters
Baking or Cake Pan (square or rectangular)	8×8×2	2 L	20×20×5
	9×9×2	2.5 L	23×23×5
	12×8×2	3 L	30×20×5
	13×9×2	3.5 L	33×23×5
Loaf Pan	8×4×3	1.5 L	20×10×7
	9×5×3	2 L	23×13×7
Round Layer Cake Pan	8×1½	1.2 L	20×4
	9×1½	1.5 L	23×4
Pie Plate	8×1¼	750 mL	20×3
	9×1¼	1 L	23×3
Baking Dish or Casserole	1 quart	1 L	—
	1½ quart	1.5 L	—
	2 quart	2 L	—